MW00424559

For 할머니

...sity Press
...1400, Downers Grove, IL 60515-1426
...m
...press.com

...y Christine Yi Suh

...ty Press® is the book-publishing division of InterVarsity Christian Fellowship/USA®, a
...of students and faculty active on campus at hundreds of universities, colleges, and
...nursing in the United States of America, and a member movement of the International
...of Evangelical Students. For information about local and regional activities, visit
...org.

...ories in this book are true, some names and identifying information may have been
...rotect the privacy of individuals.

...r cannot verify the accuracy or functionality of website URLs used in this book
...ate of publication.

...gure by InterVarsity Press
...and image composite: David Fassett
...n: Daniel van Loon
...oil background: © Katsumi Murouchi / Moment Collection /
...y Images
...r texture background: © Matthieu Tuffet / iStock / Getty Images Plus

...308-4748-8 (print)
...308-4749-5 (digital)

...United States of America ∞

...ess is committed to ecological stewardship and to the conservation of natural
...our operations. This book was printed using sustainably sourced paper.

...gress Cataloging-in-Publication Data
...d for this book is available from the Library of Congress.

8 17 16 15 14 13 12 11 10 9 8 7 6 5 4 3 2 1
6 35 34 33 32 31 30 29 28 27 26 25 24 23 22 21

CHRISTINE YI

SUZANNE STABILE, SERIE

FORTY DA

BEING A

ENNEAGRAM

InterVar
P.O. Box
ivpress.c
email@iv

©2021 b

InterVarsi
movement
schools of
Fellowship
intervarsity

All Scriptu
Internation
permission
"New Intern
Office by B

While any s
changed to p

The publish
beyond the

Enneagram
Cover design
Interior desi
Images: gold

Gett
pap

ISBN 978-0-8
ISBN 978-0-8

Printed in the

InterVarsity P
resources in al

Library of Con
A catalog recor

P   20   19

Y   38   37

An imprint of
Downers

WELCOME TO
ENNEAGRAM DAILY REFLECTIONS

Suzanne Stabile

The Enneagram is about nine ways of seeing. The reflections in this series are written from each of those nine ways of seeing. You have a rare opportunity, while reading and thinking about the experiences shared by each author, to expand your understanding of how they see themselves and how they experience others.

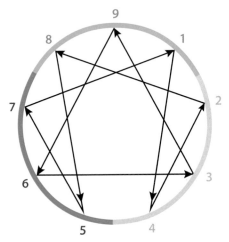

I've committed to teaching the Enneagram, in part, because I believe every person wants at least these two things: to belong, and to live a life that has meaning. And I'm sure that learning and working with the Enneagram has the potential to help all of us with both.

Belonging is complicated. We all want it, but few of us really understand it. The Enneagram identifies—with more accuracy than any other wisdom tool I know—why we can achieve belonging more easily with some people than with others. And it teaches us to find our place in situations and groups without having to displace someone else. (I'm actually convinced that it's the answer to world peace, but some have suggested that I could be exaggerating just a bit.)

If our lives are to have meaning beyond ourselves, we will have to develop the capacity to understand, value, and respect people who see the world differently than we do. We will have to learn to name our own gifts and identify our weaknesses, and the Enneagram reveals both at the same time.

The idea that we are all pretty much alike is shattered by the end of an introductory Enneagram workshop or after reading the last page of a good primer. But for those who are teachable and open to receiving Enneagram wisdom about each of the nine personality types, the shock is accompanied by a beautiful and unexpected gift: they find that they have more compassion for themselves and more grace for others and it's a guarantee.

The authors in this series, representing the nine Enneagram types, have used that compassion to move toward a greater understanding of themselves and others whose lives intersect with theirs in big and small ways. They write from experiences that reflect racial and cultural differences, and they have been influenced by their personal faith commitments. In working with spiritual directors, therapists, and pastors they identified many of their own habits and fears, behaviors and motivations, gifts and challenges. And they courageously talked with those who are close to them about how they are seen and experienced in relationship.

As you begin reading, I think it will be helpful for you to be generous with yourself. Reflect on your own life—where you've been and where you're going. And I hope you will consider the difference between change and transformation. *Change* is when we take on something new. *Transformation* occurs when something old falls away, usually beyond our control. When we see a movie, read a book, or perhaps hear a sermon that we believe "changed our lives," it will seldom, if ever, become transformative. It's a good thing and we may have learned a valuable life lesson, but that's not transformation. Transformation occurs when you have an experience that changes the way you understand life and its mysteries.

When my dad died, I immediately looked for the leather journal I had given to him years before with the request that he fill it with stories and things he wanted me to know. He had only written on one page:

> *Anything I have achieved or accomplished*
> *in my life is because of the gift of your mother*
> *as my wife. You should get to know her.*

I thought I knew her, but I followed his advice, and it was one of the most transformative experiences of my life.

From a place of vulnerability and generosity, each author in this series invites us to walk with them for forty days on their journeys toward transformation. I hope you will not limit your reading to only your number. Read about your spouse or a friend. Consider reading about the type you suspect represents your parents or your siblings. You might even want to read about someone you have little affection for but are willing to try to understand.

You can never change *how* you see, but you can change what you *do* with how you see.

ON BEING A FOUR

Welcome to *Forty Days on Being a Four*. I'm so glad you're here! You may have picked up this book because you recently discovered you are, indeed, a Four. Or maybe you were browsing online for resources on the Enneagram, and this book popped up among the other brilliant authors in the Enneagram Daily Reflections series. You might be reading this because you struggle with the Fours in your life, or you are in close relationship with a Four. Maybe you wanted to read an Enneagram book written by a woman or a person of color.

While I don't promise to explain all the dimensions of being a Four, I hope my personal reflections on family upbringing, cultural and ethnic identity, faith, justice, and spirituality will weave together universal themes of what Fours experience at our core while being shaped by our environments.

For six years I thought I was an Enneagram Two. I don't remember the exact moment when I realized I was a Four. It was more of a "trying on" than a lightbulb moment. I think many of us are mistyped by others (or by a test!), or we mistype ourselves depending on our contexts.

Part of my journey was leaving two faith communities that had shaped my acceptance of patriarchy and white supremacy. When I entered a new context where my womanhood and culture were celebrated and valued, I experienced the freedom of my true self, which matched the qualities of a Four.

I read and reread the Four descriptors in a variety of Enneagram books, devouring the content. I soon realized that the motivations of the Four reflected who I had been my whole life up to this point yet had not had permission to fully be. Examples ranged from small distinctions, such as my constant need to shape the "mood" or aesthetic of my home and workspace by lighting candles or rearranging decor (Fours see and cultivate beauty around us), to deeper issues, such as feeling like I'd never belonged anywhere (Fours grow up feeling like we are flawed). I also recognized my toxic, self-indulgent tendencies to escape the pressures of life and my way of moving toward the unhealthy patterns of a Two when I am in stress, among other patterns.

I have been on a journey of living into my Fourness for five years now, and it has been a tremendous road toward liberation and healing. At the same time, living into my true nature as a Four has come with costs. I pleased many more people as a Two and have lost friendships along the way as I became more true to my Fourness—reclaiming my needs, understanding my boundaries, and more fully living into my identity. It has also changed the way I relate to God. I no longer feel an overbearing pressure to "work for God" but instead have been leaning into enjoying God, resting in God, seeking God in both the sacred and secular.

When I first heard about the Enneagram, I found little to no literature written from the perspective of people of color. In the Enneagram trainings and workshops I attended, the nuances and realities experienced by people of color in our upbringing and spiritual formation were rarely represented. Our stories and voices seemed to be washed out and over-generalized by dominant culture voices in the Enneagram conversation. Please hear me—being a Four as a person of color doesn't make my core motivations different from my fellow Fours in dominant culture, but when we hear a singular cultural narrative about how Fours function, or how Fours came to be who they are, we ultimately dismiss or erase stories that could validate the experiences of Fours in underrepresented communities.

As a Four who is a Korean American woman, there are some things I am born in to but also some things I became as a result of my environment and experience (to really dive into this subject, see Micky ScottBey Jones's perspective in the *Sojourners* piece "The Enneagram Is Not Just for White People"). For example, since I come from a collectivistic culture, my "individualist" tendencies look different. I didn't have the freedom to explore this core aspect of myself due to cultural expectations that I would care more for my family than my own needs. It was normal for me to suppress my desires in order to honor my parents, family, and community.

Many people use the Enneagram as a way to self-actualize and become enlightened. However, this is an incomplete way of understanding the Enneagram. Yes, it is a powerful tool that sheds light on our personal growth, sense of purpose, and identity. However, the Enneagram was created *in* community and is *for* community. It is a tool that brings greater understanding, empathy, compassion, and grace to oneself and one's neighbor. We study our numbers, motivations, and behavioral patterns in order to better understand others and create a more compassionate world.

The Four tag line, "The Need to Be Special," should have been obvious to me. When I was younger I dreamed of being "the first Korean American superstar," but I never knew how to unpack that core motivation of needing to be special. I did not understand that my need to stand out came from somewhere. I now know why Mister Rogers's song "You Are Special" meant so much to me. As I have matured in my faith and self-awareness, I've realized that I am special, not because I do something to prove or show my specialness, but simply because I exist as God's beloved child.

This same reality is true for you too. I hope reading *Forty Days on Being a Four* brings you back to this truth over and over again: you are God's beloved. You are special.

ALL THE FEELS

"CHRISTINE, HOW ARE YOU FEELING?"

For years, this question has been difficult for me to answer. The more accurate question for a Four might be, "What *aren't* you feeling?"

As a Four, I store a complex universe of emotions in my inner being. When asked, "How are you doing?" I can grab my prevailing emotion and tell you how I'm doing from that emotion's point of view (joy, elation, sadness, grief, confusion —you name it!), but at any given time I live and breathe a kaleidoscope of living, feeling, conflicting emotions.

Many times Fours are labeled as "emotionally intense" or "too much," but for us it is just simply how we are. We're comfortable with liminality and in-between spaces. When Fours are healthy, our emotional state doesn't occupy anyone else's experience—instead, the multitude of emotions we carry gives us the ability to carry conflicting or contradictory emotions for others. Fours have an incredible capacity to hold space for others in paradoxical and transcendental moments. We are often invited into sacred moments (for example, the death of a loved one, the birth of a baby, transitional seasons in career, relational conflict, and so on) to help others steward these deep emotions fully.

In Luke 7:36-50, an unnamed woman comes to find Jesus. Jesus is dining at a Pharisee's home when the woman falls to the floor, begins to cry, and kisses his feet. She then pulls out a jar of expensive perfume to pour onto Jesus' feet, anointing and worshiping him in uninhibited adoration. While the Pharisees and disciples treat her with disdain because of her reputation and actions, Jesus responds with affection and esteem for her.

I love this story. Maybe it's because I like to think this unnamed woman was a Four—her creative expression in love, her unending desire to be known, her emotional rawness and intensity, and her authentic, unique way of showing up to Jesus. People misunderstood, devalued, and questioned her. The Gospel writer does not even give her name. But Jesus knew her. He dignified her and received her worship, heralding her as a faithful example for the disciples to follow.

Can you identify with the woman in this story? In what ways have you been misunderstood, devalued, or questioned by others?

Bring your weariness and exhaustion to Jesus, trusting that you can be uninhibited and unfiltered in his presence. Take some time to hear Jesus saying to you as he said to the woman, "Your faith has saved you; go in peace."

CAN YOU
UNDERSTAND ME?

TWO YEARS AGO, Sandra Oh became the first-ever Asian to be nominated for an Emmy Award as Lead Actress in a Drama Series. Oh's visibility and representation produced a groundswell of joy and pride among Asians. We rallied together to celebrate and giddily reveled in the movement as it flowed across the nation. It felt for a moment that our contributions as Asian Americans, our personhood, our stories, and our work were being seen and valued on one of the greatest platforms in the world. For me, a Korean woman like Oh, this moment felt even more specifically and directly meaningful.

Oh said something during the awards season that struck me. As she sat next to her mom at the Emmys ceremony, she said, "It's an honor just to be Asian."

It's an honor just to be Asian.

As a Four, one of my core longings and motivations is to be understood. However, my journey as a person of color living out two cultural identities compounds this innate longing. As an Asian American in this country, there are two dominant narratives our community is constantly pushing up against. We are perceived as either the *perpetual foreigner* or the *model minority*. A *perpetual* or *forever* foreigner is someone who does not belong in America, could never be born here, and does not have the right to call the United States their home. An example of this is being asked at the grocery store, "Can you speak English? *Can you understand me?*" The term *model minority* is a myth constructed by white supremacy to pit Asians against other racial groups, claiming that we naturally succeed and have somehow overcome racism through diligence and hard work. These two themes often leave us feeling generalized, diminished, and invisible.

For the majority of my life, I tried to respond to these walls of invisibility by assimilating into dominant contexts and muting my Koreanness. What I didn't realize was that in my efforts to live this way, I was not only perpetuating my people's invisibility—I was actively erasing myself, my family, and my people. My Four core need to be understood could never be met by a society resolute on diminishing and erasing my people's history and humanity.

Along my Enneagram journey, I found great comfort in the story of Hagar in the Scriptures. Hagar is an enslaved Egyptian woman who is victimized, marginalized, and deeply misunderstood. In her dual oppression, she is not *seen* in her context. Hagar is impregnated by her owner,

Abram, and subsequently experiences the devastating loss of her home and community. In Genesis 16, Hagar flees into the desert, and in this moment of great vulnerability, God pursues her. God seeks to understand her and asks, "Where have you come from, and where are you going?" As Hagar engages God, she becomes the first person in the Bible to name God. She calls out to God as "El Roi, the God who sees me."

In my longing as a Four to be understood, I wonder to myself how I, like Hagar, can be set free from societal narratives that claim I can be only a model minority or a perpetual foreigner. Instead of yielding to these portrayals by the dominant culture, how can I show up fully in the unique way I've been created? God is the God who sees, but I am also a part of making God visible to the world.

As a Korean American woman, my story is connected to generations of ancestors before me who also resisted narratives meant to perpetuate self-hatred in people of color. My story is woven into the fabric of my Asian American sisters, mothers, daughters, and grandmothers who reclaimed their dignity in the face of oppression. I no longer see my Koreanness as something to be hidden, diminished, or erased but am learning to stand fully on the sacred and holy ground of being an Asian American woman. I bear the extraordinary image of God, and in choosing to embrace where I've come from and where I am going, I can't help but feel these same words: "It's an honor just to be Asian."

Reflect on your story and the intersectional identities you hold. What does it mean to you that God is El Roi, the God who sees you?

If you are a Four and experience a desire to be understood, what does it mean that you make God visible to the world?

Take some time to respond to the question that God asks Hagar: "Where have you come from, and where are you going?"

AM I NORMAL?

FOURS TYPICALLY GROW UP FEELING that there is something different, something flawed inside us. We never feel as though we truly belong or are understood, and in turn, internalize a belief that there is something wrong with us. We think our differences from others disqualify or separate us from relationships, opportunities, growth, and community.

Because of this, I have asked myself one question over and over throughout my life: "Is this normal? Am I normal? Am I OK?"

Lately I've been thinking about individuals in the Scriptures who were marginalized and seen only for their flaws. I see how Jesus consistently models an upside-down kingdom, embodying the expansive love of God by drawing close to them.

In John 4, Jesus crosses religious and cultural boundaries to travel through Samaria and approaches a woman at a well. In this woman's story we see how Jesus reaches across gender, culture, and religion to welcome her fully. The woman goes home to tell others of the good news that has liberated and healed her. "Come, see a man who told me everything I ever did. Could this be the Messiah?"

Even the disciples are perplexed by what Jesus does, but his actions speak loud and clear. This woman is seen, known, and worthy of being accepted into the kingdom of God.

I am burdened by the many souls who, like the woman at the well, have been made to ask themselves, "Am I normal?" or "Am I OK?" after being harmed or rejected by the church. Many faith communities perpetuate oppressive and violent environments for Black, indigenous, and other people of color; women; the LGBTQIA community; people with disabilities; immigrants; and other marginalized communities. Out of fear and a sense of scarcity, the church builds theological walls that label and categorize instead of humanizing tables that embrace and dignify.

The late Rachel Held Evans, in her book *Searching for Sunday*, aptly describes God's kingdom as "a bunch of outcasts and oddballs gathered at a table, not because they are rich or worthy or good, but because they are hungry, because they said yes. And there's always room for more." May we know that there is always room for more in the economy of God.

Think about something in your life that causes deep shame or amplifies your perceived "flaws." Imagine God seeking you out as he did the woman at the well, speaking to you in deep love and radical acceptance. Rest in the abundant, compassionate love God has for you, just as you are.

COCOONING AND THE INNER VOICE

AT THE BEGINNING OF THIS YEAR, I embarked on a journey inward. As a Four, I have found that solitude and contemplation are lifelines in sustaining authenticity in my spiritual life and in grounding me toward the work of justice. Solitude allows me to attend to the sound of God's voice within while uprooting narratives of internalized oppression and removing the barriers of noise and distraction.

Early in the year I made the difficult decision to step down from my pastoral position and leave my church community. I knew it would take time to heal from the loss of dreams, relationships, and a place of spiritual belonging. I began bracing myself for a season of "cocooning"—deliberately clearing my schedule and paying attention only to who and what was right in front of me: my family and my soul. There was nothing to do, nowhere to go; I had only to simply be.

For the previous three and a half years as a pastor, I had become used to overextending outward expressions of spirituality. In my outward-facing role, I had become more and more internally compartmentalized, stretched thin from being pulled in many directions. My commitment to contemplative practice and spiritual disciplines began to wane and I felt a subtle but serious change in my spirit. It was getting harder and harder to access my interior life, the "sound of the genuine" within me named by Howard Thurman in his Spellman College commencement address in 1980.

Authenticity for me as a Four means I need to be in touch with my interior life. And in this season, facing the state of my spiritual health meant owning the truth that I could no longer hear the sound of the voice within. My soul was desperately in need of space to exhale.

When I announced my departure, several concerned friends, colleagues, and family members tried to console me. "Don't worry—God has a plan for you." "When God closes a door, another one will always open!" Some even used my "cocooning" analogy to tell me how excited they were that I was about to become a butterfly. But the truth is, I was not interested in metamorphosis. I had no desire to fly—I was exhausted with "doing" and simply wanted to "be."

In this set apart time and space, I have been searching for that inner voice, the place where I know the Spirit of God is living, breathing, and calling for me. I am slowing down in order to become whole again. The "cocooning" is a time for reflection and healing, putting back together what has become fractured or fragmented. In order to heal myself, I am actively seeking God in the *being*, not the *doing*.

What are ways you can cultivate solitude and tend to the voice of God within you?

Allow these words from mystic Teresa of Avila's *Interior Castle* to encourage you in your journey inward:

> There is a secret place. A radiant sanctuary. As real as your own kitchen. More real than that. Constructed of the purest elements. Overflowing with the ten thousand beautiful things. Worlds within worlds. . . . This magnificent refuge is inside you. Enter. Shatter the darkness that shrouds the doorway. . . . Step around the poisonous vipers that slither at your feet, attempting to throw you off your course. Be bold. Be humble. Put away the incense and forget the incantations they taught you. Ask no permission from the authorities. Slip away. Close your eyes and follow your breath to the still place that leads to the invisible path that leads you home. . . . Believe the incredible truth that the Beloved has chosen for his dwelling place the core of your own being because that is the single most beautiful place in all of creation.

Take some time this week to schedule uninterrupted time to listen to the sound of the genuine within you.

ORIGINALITY

IN COLLEGE, MY PEERS OFTEN had impassioned conversations about their calling and how they were going to change the world. I was envious of their certainty and sense of purpose. My friend Steph became a social justice warrior, Marshall a teacher, Sarah a filmmaker, Wend a lawyer. But what was my calling? Why was I lacking in these early decisions for choosing my future vocation?

I can see now that my Fourness contributed to my inability to commit. Even if I were to confine myself to one thing, ultimately I didn't want to fit into a singular box. The pressure to conform into one career path and meet those social expectations suffocated me. I avoided defining myself with one avenue of expression and comically changed my major six times. However, looking back, these actions were rooted in an anchoring, marvelous belief within me: "I am an original." Cue Leslie Odom Jr. singing "Wait for It" from the musical *Hamilton*.

The authors of *Spiritual Rhythms for the Enneagram* say that for Fours, "Creativity joyfully renews." Now, well into my thirties, I realize as a Four, creating is part of my DNA. And this is an ever-evolving process! When I am at my healthiest, I don't take myself too seriously. Because I move to One in security, I anchor myself in One-like qualities of focused determination, responsibility, precision, and integrity. I don't compare myself to others, and I soar high above criticism.

Rather than finding my calling, my calling continues to find me. My calling is not static or fixed. It is an endless constellation of possibilities to create, build, shape, form, and originate. My calling is part of God's ever-expanding movement of healing in individuals, communities, and our world through creative expression.

As a singer, I see an awakening of humanity as a series of notes in harmony or in cacophony. Major and minor notes carving a path for courageous dissidence over conformity, crescendos of ever-changing possibility, promise, and deliverance. When I sing, I feel the Spirit of God soaring hope through my vocal chords.

As a painter, I see time and space—past, present, and future—as a series of brush strokes on canvas: layers of circumstances, events, and relationships building atop each other; patterns unveiling new roads to travel; a vivid blending of communities creating purposeful connection and vision. When I paint, I sense God's loving hand blending colorful textures of humanity and compassion.

When I write or preach, a supernatural boldness and clarity washes over me to pierce an empty space with words of redemption and reclamation. Giving others the ability to reimagine a new way connects me to the Divine—a way of seeing, being, knowing, and living.

As a mother, friend, wife, sister, auntie, and daughter—as an Asian American woman—I see my existence as an act of resistance. A revelation of creative exploration and articulation. New trails to blaze, unfound paths to carve for the generations before, beside, and behind me.

To change the world, I must be originally me.

What has been your journey to discovering your calling? If you are a Four, do you find yourself confined by a singular role, title, responsibility, or position?

Reflect on Adele Calhoun's insights that for Fours, "creativity joyfully renews." How does this mantra speak to you?

PRACTICE MAKES PROGRESS

WHEN I WAS GROWING UP, my family and I would look forward to the figure skating competitions every Winter Olympics. We would cheer for our favorites, holding our breath while the athletes performed thrilling jumps and graceful spins. One particular winter, in 1998, I saw seventeen-year-old Michelle Kwan for the first time. She looked just like me! She had my skin tone and my hair and she was tiny, just like my middle school self at the time. To top it off, she was amazing on the ice!

Whenever I saw her skate, I was changed. I would cease being Christine and slowly embody being Michelle. In my living room and backyard and garage, I would practice and practice being like her. Of course, I didn't know how to ice skate, but I did have a fierce pair of rollerblades. I rallied all my friends at church and hosted skating competitions in our parking garage. I practiced my triple axel, my double toe loop, my sit spin, my signature spiral. There was no one like

Michelle on the ice! And there was no one like Christine in a parking garage.

During those winter seasons, I would daydream about becoming a famous ice skater like Kwan. Even though I had no access to an ice skating rink, I'd fantasize about becoming the next great ice skating representation for Asian Americans in the United States. As a Four, I've always had grandiose fantasies about what I could achieve or become, and when I look back, I see the many different paths I anticipated success in, whether it was in sports, academics, music—or ice skating!

Fours are known to be idealistic dreamers who envision powerful, creative ways of contributing to the world. And yet Fours also have a pattern of avoiding the actual work needed to fulfill these dreams. In our search for significance and meaning, we get paralyzed by the internal pressure to be more than we actually believe we can be.

Now that I'm in my thirties, I've learned that I need to take the pressure off of myself to perform, to be the most unique, or to be more than I actually am. The appropriate phrase isn't "practice makes perfect" for Fours—it's "practice makes progress."

> What comes up within you when you hear the phrase "practice makes progress"? If you're a Four, do you relate to having grandiose fantasies about your unique contributions to the world? What are some ways you've "practiced" in order to make progress on these dreams? Write out an action plan for making progress on your dream.

PEGGED AS A TWO

WHEN I LEFT MY SEMINARY STUDIES in Massachusetts and moved back home to California, I was in search of a new spiritual director. After months of looking, I was excited to secure an appointment with a vetted, reputable director who specialized in the Enneagram.

It was a bright and early morning when I walked into the small brick-stone chapel where we had decided to meet. A promising light shone through the colorful mosaic glass windows. I was eager to start our session.

However, after our initial introductions, the director, a white woman, said, "I have another Korean female client who is a Two-Wing Three, and you remind me so much of her."

I began to share my story with her, and she continued to associate me with the aforementioned client. From what she had gathered about "the pressures of Korean culture," she projected that I had a tendency to serve others and find worth in performance. For the next hour she evaluated me and delegated me as a Two-Wing Three. My body was tense the entire hour of our meeting as I nodded and tried to smile. However, instead of resisting her words, I internalized them.

At the time, I didn't see the director's behavior as problematic. I didn't have the language or tools to understand why I felt my body tighten up in her analysis of me. Now I understand that she was directing me with racial bias and stereotypical narratives.

In the book *Kaleidoscope,* minister and spiritual director Ruth Takiko West discusses this common experience shared by people of color in dominant contexts: "Unless [spiritual leaders] are sensitive to the lived realities of nondominant culture people, the hospitality that is offered may be more stifling than respiting, more harm than blessing."

Well-meaning people can be the most oblivious to this. Even if it was not the director's intent to harm me, I was being triggered by the microaggressions in her assumptions about my story, my culture, and who I was. Yet here's the dilemma I faced: She had training and knowledge about the Enneagram that I didn't; therefore, I should trust her assessment—shouldn't I?

I wish I could say I listened to my body, which was pleading with me to get up and get out of that room. Instead I did what I was used to doing my whole life in dominant contexts. I disembodied myself, pushed out my lived experience as a Korean woman, and accepted her evaluation as right and true. For the next six years, I believed I was a Two-Wing Three.

In the early stages of your Enneagram journey, were you pegged as another number by an authority figure you trusted or respected? Or perhaps you've had a friend, colleague, or family member mistype you.

Oftentimes the intersecting lines of religion, culture, and gender greatly impact the way we are perceived. Take some time now to acknowledge and grieve, if needed, the ways that these relationships or individuals caused harm (intentional or not) to you. Imagine Jesus consoling you, keeping you safe, and loving you just as you are.

TAKE UP SPACE

IT WAS MY FIRST DAY as a pastor at my church, and my colleague (and now good friend) Katie was giving me a tour of the campus. Our church was leasing a large high school from the local school district, and the sanctuary was an auditorium that held close to three thousand people.

After the tour, Katie and I stepped outside to greet congregants who were slowly trickling in. I knew service was starting soon and wanted to check my phone to see what time it was. As I looked around, I realized I had left my purse in the sanctuary, and I hurriedly flung open the backdoor to run through the dimly lit backstage. The worship band was still practicing their set when I ran past the curtains onto the stage.

I froze in horror as I realized the band wasn't practicing—they were actually leading the congregation in worship! Service had started. I want to emphasize again that I did not cautiously tiptoe onto the stage; I torpedoed my way up there to the shock of, well, everyone.

So there I was, my very first Sunday, already engaging in my first literal misstep—a very big and irreversible misstep. I locked eyes with our worship director, Markay, who with distress in his eyes signaled to me that this was a mistake. I quickly nodded my head in agreement and eased back into the shadows from whence I came.

Thinking about this story always makes me laugh. It's one of those most embarrassing moments I can recall in great detail, a story I like to share with friends. But this story is also a reminder of the ways Fours often feel about being on stage or in the spotlight, whether literally or figuratively, in our lives as creatives and individuals.

Fours feel a burning brilliance within that wants to shine, yet at the same time, deep down we are skeptical about our talent. We grapple with the desire to share our gifts, yet we are unsure if what we have to offer is valuable. On one level, women already deal with this dilemma in male-dominated contexts when they grapple with imposter syndrome. For women of color, the uncertainty is even more layered and nuanced. As a Four who is also a woman of color, all of these dynamics coexist, causing me to wonder, *Can I take up this space? Am I allowed to be here?*

In the Netflix documentary *Knock Down the House*, first-time congressional candidate Alexandria Ocasio-Cortez is about to debate longstanding incumbent Joe Crowley, whom she would ultimately unseat. As she prepares her speech in the safety of her home, she begins to speak words of life, takes deep breaths, and centers herself. She spreads her arms and waves them to fill the room: "I need to take up space. . . . I need to take up space."

You are invited to take up space.

> Take some time to practice taking up space right where you are. Be mindful of your body taking up the space around you. Open your arms wide and take several deep breaths. Release your inhibitions and feel the freedom to move around where you are. Take up the space and speak words of life to yourself! No need to shrink, diminish, or hide. Know that you are enough, you shine, you bear the image of God in the way only you can!

GROWING OUR SOULS

IN MY FAITH TRADITION, I was taught that silence is one of the main streams for seeking God. I trained for years to seek out silence so I could cultivate an inner life of prayer. As a Four, I invested time in this quiet space, seeking authentic experiences with God. But these days I have been seeing silence differently.

As I write this, our country is in the midst of a renewed revolution for Black lives. Yet amid this reckoning, I'm seeing how silence is being used (in the name of Jesus) to further oppress and harm our Black siblings. I see leaders in our government and media silence oppressed communities. I see dominant culture hide behind silence in order to ignore and invalidate the humanity and pain of the marginalized. I see the church perpetuate and propagandize violence and murder against Black and Brown communities with its silence.

Many of us are finally opening our eyes to see the evils of racial hierarchy and white supremacy. Our nation's deep-rooted, widespread, and wicked systemic atrocities against the Black community have led to mass incarcerations, lack of equity across institutions, disproportionate access to healthcare, and state-sanctioned violence and murder. Since the founding of our nation, white supremacy has festered and flared as the Black community has suffered and endured —and we have remained silent. Our silence is an assault on our Black siblings.

Fours often feel a pressure to give up parts of ourselves in order to belong. We experience tension when it comes to speaking out or staying silent in matters of justice because we've carefully cultivated an identity around being accepted by those proximate to us. However, our nation's racial reckoning must wake us up to those crying out for justice. These times call for us to break any mold we've superficially fit into for acceptance. These times call for courageous creativity and leadership.

Silence may be a spiritual practice, but it is also a tool for violent oppression. If in our "thoughts and prayers" we can't hear the noise—the moans, the cries, the weeping of our Black siblings—our spiritual silence may be a coping mechanism for maintaining our own privilege. If from our prayers we are not compelled to speak out and take action, our spiritual silence is tantamount to apathetic gluttony. Like theologian James Cone has said, "Silence in the face of innocent suffering is complicity in the act itself."

When Fours are in health, we integrate toward One (Reformer) characteristics. We move away from our own self-absorption and synthesize our creativity alongside a call to justice and humanity. We channel our disposition for authenticity to challenge the ways the church can be faithful in our call "to act justly and to love mercy and to walk humbly with [our] God" (Micah 6:8).

If we look at the life of Jesus, we see that genuine experiences in silence and prayer call us into the noise, chaos, and messiness of the work of justice. Genuine spiritual experiences are catalysts for transformation and activism—both individually and societally. A genuine pursuit of God moves us to action—we leave behind a cheap, individualized, self-interested faith for a deeper, complex, communal faith that seeks the acknowledgement and care for all.

Asian American activist Grace Lee Boggs said, "These are the times to grow our souls. Each of us is called upon to embrace the conviction that despite the powers and principalities bent on commodifying all our human relationships, we have the power within us to create the world anew." As people of faith, solitude and silence must move us to stand in solidarity with the oppressed. In doing so, we join a great cloud of witnesses—activists, teachers, leaders and students—ordinary people across generations who gave their lives for a future unrealized but hoped for. We are being invited to grow our souls.

If you are a Four, what is your relationship with silence, prayer, justice, and activism? What would it look like to "grow your soul" by standing against anti-Blackness, in solidarity with the oppressed, and joining in the work to dismantle systemic racism?

Therese Taylor-Stinson says, "All contemplation should be followed by action; they are there for one another. The reason to contemplate anything would be to have clarity about what action to take next." As a Four, how can you better integrate your experiences of contemplation and action?

LORD! LORD! LORD!

FOR AS LONG AS I CAN REMEMBER, the Korean church has hosted prayer at early dawn. When I was growing up, our church was a thirty-minute drive from our house, which meant we had to leave no later than four-thirty in the morning. I remember the biting cold as my mom whipped off my blanket to wake me. I would beg for an extra minute or two as I curled my body into a fetal position. Half-awake, my sister and I would groggily put on layers of sweaters and fumble into the car, falling back asleep only to be woken again, this time to enter the church building.

Promptly at five, the pastor would invite the congregation into *Tongsun Kido*. *Tongsung* means "crying out together loudly," and *Kido* means "prayer." My parents would get on their knees, lift up their arms, and begin to cry out, "*Joo Yoh! Joo Yoh! Joo Yoh!*" meaning "Lord! Lord! Lord!" If my sister and I had once again fallen asleep, the loud wailing, moaning, and cries would jolt us awake again for the final time. No one could sleep through *Tongsun Kido*.

In this place, as the sun began to color the skies with its yellow and orange strokes, my parents prayed earnestly, their emotions uninhibited and raw. They cried out their prayers until their voices were hoarse, meditatively rocking back and forth into a contemplative state. They then began to mutter words beneath their breath, as though they were being calmed in God's embrace.

When I reach back into these childhood memories, I realize that these early dawn prayer meetings were my first experiences of contemplation and lament. Watching my parents cry out in need, longing, desperation, and hope shaped me profoundly as a Four. In a culture of saving face and navigating shame and honor, this was one of the few spaces where one could exhale from pressure and performance and simply lament. *Tongsun Kido* bore the pain of a marginalized community; there was no room for superficial religiosity. I believe that many of us in Western culture long for an outlet for our lament.

As a Four, I have found the spiritual practice of lament to be critical to my own maturity and healing. Oftentimes I find myself getting caught in a cycle of sadness with no outlet. Fours carry feelings of melancholy, grief, and loss, and the weight of the world can bear heavily on our shoulders. If we don't have a landing place to release these weighty feelings, we lose ourselves to our emotions.

Lament is a powerful avenue for relief, closure, and hope for a Four. It may take a different shape from the *Tongsun*

Kido my parents modeled to me early on, but it is still necessary. The practice of honest confession, dependence, and need is a belief that God can bring change, hope, and restoration to our souls and circumstances.

Read Psalm 142. Spend some time journaling about your moments of grief and pain in the last month or so—bring those emotions before God and imagine Jesus grieving alongside you. As the psalmist says, cry loud to God. Share your troubles with God, pour out your heart, and allow God to watch over you.

SPIRITUAL DIRECTION

THERE IS A PHOTO ON MY WALL above my desk of the path leading up to my spiritual director's home. She lives in a hilly area that overlooks the city—a sacred place of retreat and withdrawal. Jane is a constant person in my life, a pastoral presence committed to entering into the deepest spaces of my soul together with me.

As a Four, I was used to navigating my motivations, contradictions, relationships, spirituality, and sense of calling on my own. I took deep pride in being self-aware and having tools to untangle interwoven complexities in my inner world. However, this all came to a head several years ago when I had my first child. In the first nine months of becoming a new mom, my life became clouded by doubt, despair, and hopelessness. No matter how many pastoral meetings, therapy sessions, or discipleship/mentoring conversations I engaged in, I was mired in despondency.

Barbara Brown Taylor, in *Learning to Walk in the Dark*, says we often seek pastors, mentors, and counselors when we "want help getting out of caves," but we go to spiritual directors when we are "ready to be led farther in." Spiritual direction became one of the main ways I sought, as a Four, to be led further into God's presence.

For some, going into a dark or uncertain place may feel unnecessary or strange. But we Fours are up for the challenge. We are not afraid to see what's inside the cave. We want to know what resides within, even if we don't like what we find. We need to explore our inner complexity, even if what we discover involves holding multiple realities together all at once. There is great comfort in knowing we do not have to make this discovery alone—someone skilled and gifted at noticing the sacred can make the journey restorative, fun, and grounding.

My spiritual director has been a counselor—a flashlight guiding me to explore the untraveled places of my soul, reassuring me through my fear that God is with me. She has been a comforting blanket that doubles as a hardy backpack, providing me with a resting place yet wisely equipping me with the tools to cultivate my inner life. She's been an oxygen mask to revive me in moments of breathlessness and an anchor that keeps me steadfast in stormy waters. She has been a "midwife for my soul," as Margaret Guenther puts it. More than her presence, personhood, or giftings, it has been the practice of spiritual direction—engaging an ongoing rhythm of purposefully giving attention to God—that has mattered most.

The true Director, the Spirit of God, covers and hovers over our time, providing space for honest reflection, lament, and joy, waiting in the stillness. My soul is safe.

> What has been your relationship with spiritual direction? How do you (or how might you) benefit from a partner and guide who helps tend to your soul and inner being?

GARAGE SALE

ABOUT A YEAR AGO, my parents hosted a massive garage sale in their front yard. They had talked about it for years, ever since my sister and I moved out of the house, but it just never happened. There was an area of the garage that was full of relics of our past—old VHS tapes, yearbooks, even clothing that hadn't been touched in over ten years.

My parents intentionally didn't invite my sister or me because it was one of those hurtful garage sales—they were selling our childhood keepsakes and memories! There was so much stuff accumulated over thirty-plus years that my parents didn't even go through it; they simply dumped our possessions onto the front yard, posted a Craigslist ad, and waited for people to come.

Like most immigrant families, my family saved everything anyone ever gave us. They had been in survival mode for so long that they didn't throw anything away. Did we need scratched-up, dusty, "vintage" Corelle plates? Yes. Did we need twenty mismatched blankets, covers, and pillow sets? Of course. Did we need to keep old and outdated routers, computers, and printers? Absolutely, because they probably still worked. And we without a doubt needed all of our old high school textbooks and decades-old encyclopedias because, well, they were full of important information.

When I found out early that morning what my parents were doing, I grabbed my spouse and forced him to come along to make sure they weren't getting rid of any treasures. It was an overwhelming scene. A mountain of ancient furniture, fatigued cookware, heavily creased J. T. T. (Jonathan Taylor Thomas) and H.O.T. (Highfive of Teenagers) posters, scratched-up nineties DVDs and sad-looking VHS tapes, faded K-Pop CD covers (most missing the actual CDs), creased books for all ages, clothing, shoes . . . I was in shock. Our stuff spilled over from the yard onto the sidewalk of my parents' and bordering neighbors' homes. It looked like our own version of Korean *American Pickers*.

Even though I'm poking fun at my parents for accumulating so many material things over all those years, in a similar way, I've held onto piles of emotional baggage as a Four and let that burden completely guide my life. I have a cabinet of memories filed away of people who have hurt or harmed me. In times of stress or vulnerability, I replay negative episodes from my past and reopen wounds as if I might find greater self-realization on the other side. Of course, these anticipated epiphanies never materialize.

But these days I'm trying to break the cycle—I want to have my own garage sale of sorts. As I tiptoe toward my thirty-fifth birthday this year, I'm realizing I cannot continue to live in insecurity and self-rejection. I am working toward absolving others of their control over me and allowing God to fill in the spaces that are vulnerable. My worth is not confined to the ever-changing noise and opinions of other people, but rather it is grounded in the steady quiet of God's unconditional love.

If you are a Four or in relationship with a Four, do you hold onto emotional or relational baggage? How do you move on after believing your identity is based on your feelings about a negative situation or relationship?

FRIENDSHIP WITH GOD

FOURS EXTEND AUTHENTICITY and empathy in friendships and seek deep connection with others. We are among the most emotionally intuitive Enneagram types, yet long for reciprocal spaces that don't require us to diminish our inner complexities.

Early in my faith development, my church leaders consistently emphasized two main ways of growing in our relationship with God: serving the church and knowing correct doctrine. I dove deeply into both pools, and my main mode of engaging God became *working* for God and *knowing* about God. These two endeavors would become my primary form of discipleship in my adult years, even influencing my decision to do postgraduate work in theology.

I was in my midtwenties when, over a cup of coffee, a mentor of mine asked about my friendship with God. The question caught me off guard. I told him I didn't really have one, that God was more like a holy "Other" to me.

He then asked me, "When is the last time you remember enjoying God?" The question was all at once so strange, so surprising, yet so relieving that I began to cry.

To be honest, I hadn't really thought God was enjoyable up to that point. I knew God was loving and cared about me, but I'd always felt a barrier between us. My mentor went on to say that more than my "work" for God, God wanted to know *me*.

"Well, how do I begin?" I asked.

He said the ingredients of a healthy friendship were the same ingredients in one's relationship with God. We started to discuss what made a friendship healthy: self-revelation, honesty, reciprocity, quality time, consistency of communication, and shared interests.

It was a profound moment to realize that God wanted to see me for who I truly was, not for the work or theology I was producing. As a Four, it was deeply comforting to realize that God wants to come close to me just as I am. I didn't need to diminish parts of myself or strive to be more in order to gain intimacy and friendship. I was being invited to move from a transactional relationship with God to a transformational one—one of healing, rest, collaboration, and enjoyment.

If you are a Four, what would it look like for you to begin a healing journey of friendship with God?

Imagine Jesus saying to you, "I do not call you servants any longer. . . . I have called you friends" (John 15:15). What comes up within you as you read those words?

What does it mean for you that God longs to come close to you, just as you are, right where you are?

A CALLING

AS A FOUR, I HAVE EXPENDED extraordinary emotional energy carving my own path. I have always struggled with finding worth through others' opinions or expectations of me. At the same time, I longed to be true to myself and struggled with feeling like I didn't fit the mold that had been set for me.

Growing up in the Korean immigrant church, I was surrounded by leadership models where only men pastored and preached over adults. I had no problem with it at the time—it was what was taught and modeled to me, and the only way I knew. But during my senior year in college, I started paying attention to my passion for ministry, theology, and a longing to study the Bible. I wanted to give my life to God and gain tools to guide others in the faith.

When I told my parents and church community I wanted to go to seminary, they asked, "What will you do after you get your degree? What is it you want to do?" I didn't have a response for them then but looking back now, if I had had the imagination for it, if some kind of paradigm had given me permission for it, I would have said with honesty: "I want to be a pastor."

Throughout my life, I had felt a holy fire within me to minister, shepherd, and lead. However, I had been taught women could not be pastors. Children's rights activist Marian Wright Edelman is often quoted saying, "You can't be what you can't see," and this was my reality. I had never seen someone who looks or sounds like me preach, teach, or lead in the way that I felt I was being called to. I was uncertain and terrified to even explore the possibility.

Yet over time I began to take seriously what I felt God's Spirit was stirring up within me. One day, when a friend strongly encouraged me to apply for a pastoral position at her church, I heard an invitation from God to embark on a new journey. I pursued the pastorate wholeheartedly and began to exercise my gifts in their fullness. As a Four, I constantly struggled with feeling flawed. But my authentic self was coming alive in ways I had never encountered before. I was experiencing a newfound brilliance and boldness burning with me! It was as though I was shedding an old self bound by systems that couldn't contain me. I was becoming a more whole version of who God made me to be.

It's now been four years since I have lived fully into my pastoral call. If I had stayed within the boundary lines of what was expected of me or listened to others' opinions, my family and I would have missed out on God's invitation of grace! We look back on our journey and cannot help but declare with mother Mary, "Nothing is impossible with God!" (Luke 1:37).

If you are a Four, what has been an experience where you have had to carve your own path?

How do you relate to a sense of longing for something?

COLD NOODLES

FOURS TEND TO ROMANTICIZE THE PAST. As a daughter of immigrants, I tend to do this as a form of both gratitude and survivor's guilt; it's a way to cope with the weight of sacrifice my family endured.

My parents owned and operated a small Korean restaurant that specialized in cold noodles, or *nengmyun*, for close to twenty years. The restaurant changed locations a few times, from Garden Grove to Los Angeles, finally ending up in a strip mall on the corner of Third and Ardmore in Koreatown. My father's mother had passed away earlier that year, and in remembrance, my parents hung up a large portrait of my grandmother imprinted with our family's story—our legacy. The recipe for my grandmother's noodles originated in Ham Hung City in the northern part of Korea, where she grew up. When she immigrated to the United States, she brought along her recipes, intertwined with memories of home.

My dad was the restaurant's chef. He took immense pride in his noodle-making technique, his hands a canvas of the years they endured, scarred and stiffened with wear. His knuckles are comically large, his forearms disfigured with scars and burns in honor of the busiest days of the year when kitchen temperatures soared over ninety degrees. The creases on my mother's face, on her brows and around her mouth, are a testament to her grit in managing the front of the restaurant; she shouldered the weight of her lifeline with a determined smile every day.

The restaurant was closed only one day of the year: New Year's Day. My family spent many birthdays, Mother's Days, Thanksgivings, and Christmases at the restaurant, and my sister and I were expected to help out as waitresses and busboys, washing the dishes and filling empty water cups. I think of all the momentous occasions we spent at the restaurant, and although I was bitter about spending those special days there when I was young, today my soul aches with gratitude as I see the decades of sacrifice worn on my parents' bodies. My parents' prime years have come and gone, and now they are gray-haired with wrinkled skin. But there is no regret. "We were able to give our daughters every opportunity," they would say. "What is there to regret?"

As a Four, I often long to relive the past. I imagine going back in time and watching my father carefully prepare each dish in the sweltering heat of our restaurant kitchen. I envision sitting at a restaurant booth and taking in my mother's gracious bow to each customer walking through our doors. When I close my eyes, I look into their eyes and hold their hands. I grasp the gravity of what they were doing for my sister and me in the daily, hourly, minute-by-minute overflow of love. In their sacrifice, they embodied Jesus' words for us: "This is my body, broken for you." A legacy of pouring out, a life of sacrifice, faith, and devotion.

> Think of someone who has loved you into being, who has sacrificed deeply on your behalf. Take some time to thank God for their life and be present to your gratitude. Become aware of God's loving presence.
>
> Imagine Jesus saying these words to you: "This is my body given for you. . . . This cup is the new covenant in my blood, which is poured out for you" (Luke 22:19-20). Give thanks to God, and ask how and where in your life you may "lay down your life" in sacrifice for others.

A DISINTEGRATED FOUR

BEING A TWO (THE HELPER) made sense, really. As a Korean woman, I fit neatly into the Twolike qualities that the dominant culture expected of me and that were approved of in my church tradition, so it almost seemed right.

To be successful at my Korean church, I molded myself as someone "behind the scenes" or "helpful" to support the men in prominent roles. Although I have deep love and fondness for this community that raised me, my peers and I were shaped by a religious culture built on a hierarchy of patriarchy.

In white-dominant spaces, I mastered the unspoken rules, still striving to utilize my gifts within the boundary lines. I shrank myself to fit into tokenized roles or sought permission to exist in boxes that were never made for women of color. Even if the words "You cannot lead" were not directly spoken, the message was clear in both of these environments—in the teaching and preaching of the church, within the broader culture of white supremacy and misogyny, and in seeing who was represented in senior leadership and administrative bodies.

Over time I came to imagine that I was someone who could *help* but not *lead*. I could *support* but not *create*. I could dream but only for someone else's dream.

As I learned more about the Enneagram, my teachers taught me that each type moves in the direction of integration and growth when healthy and in the direction of disintegration when under stress. When Fours move toward growth, we embody healthy One (Reformer) characteristics: we are self-disciplined, responsible, organized, and focused on a greater vision to heal the world. However, when Fours are in disintegration, we move in the direction of an unhealthy Two, employing people-pleasing, manipulative, clingy behaviors to prove our worthiness.

An unfortunate and detrimental consequence of my environmental upbringing was that I was celebrated for my qualities as a disintegrated Four. I perpetuated unhealthy patterns and boundaries—I tried to become the ideal helper, someone who was there for everyone. I mastered people-pleasing and strove to be a necessary fixture that no one could abandon. I strove to be special by being needed, and time and time again I was praised by my superiors and peers for my overproducing, overhelping, and overextending. The deep anxiety, fragmentation, and stress I carried during those years was a sign that I needed help. The worth I was searching for could never be fulfilled as an unrealized Four.

In our Enneagram journeys, understanding our movements toward disintegration and integration is a pivotal step toward self-awareness, self-acceptance, growth, and maturity. But more significantly, these powerful revelations allow us to live into greater healing and wholeness.

What has it looked like for your Enneagram type to function in disintegration or integration?

Take some time to think about how your religious and cultural upbringings have shaped you. If you are a Four, how are you living into greater healing, maturity, and wholeness?

FOGGY VISION

IN THE EARLY YEARS OF MY MARRIAGE, I worked at a college near the Pacific coastline where a sudden fog rolling in from the ocean was a common occurrence. Sometimes I'd be met with this fog unexpectedly while driving early in the morning or late at night. The sudden lack of visibility required an immediate and complete adjustment. The fog was so thick I would have to slow my speed and turn on my fog lights, and I felt as though I was driving in unknown territory. I may have driven this particular road for years, but I could no longer see the entire path. I needed to trust what I knew of the road before the fog arrived.

As with many Fours, I have struggled with depression for most of my life. Even when things were going really well, the pressures and pulls of life at various points throughout the years created a foggy haze that was difficult to navigate. I could hardly see through these trying times, much less walk through them. The fogginess of these episodes was compounded by my need to pull away and self-isolate.

I started experiencing depressive symptoms as a young college student. As a child of Asian immigrants, I had no framework for understanding or dealing with mental health issues. I struggled through these valleys alone, flexing my Three wing to try to press through until I felt "normal." I confronted these episodes by taking on more responsibilities in an effort to "fix" myself. I didn't think to reach out to anyone or try to share what I was going through.

Even though I shared many intimate things about myself to my dearest, closest friends, the fog was off-limits. I wanted help, but I believed at the time that depression was not an illness; it was a byproduct of not working hard enough. I had seen my parents endure and survive emotional trauma time and time again. I just needed to push through and push harder for survival.

I was pregnant with my second child a year after my son was born when I spiraled into deep postpartum depression. My emotions felt out of control and I could no longer ignore or invalidate the feelings of sadness and isolation. The pressures of being a full-time working mother, wife, friend, and leader in ministry began to pile up, and things came to a head when I experienced a breakdown during a work trip. Out of desperation, I committed to meeting regularly with a therapist and spiritual director.

It has now been seven years since I began regularly seeking mental, spiritual, and emotional support in managing my depression. Instead of brushing my emotions

58

away, I've grown to practice self-compassion and self-love. I have also opened myself up to asking for and receiving help from loved ones. Intentionally embracing the whole me takes daily practice and grace. And although the fog is and will be a constant in my life, I'm seeing more clearly and walking more fully than I ever have before.

> Fours feel emotions very deeply, and many of us have regular experiences with melancholy. If you're a Four or in a relationship with a Four, what are some ways you are paying attention to mental and emotional health? What are some practices that bring healing and restoration to your soul?

FEELING ALONE

AS A CHILD, I WAS TERRIFIED OF THE DARK. I had a wild imagination, and every night I would dread going to bed. I'd beg my mom and dad to stay with me or ask if I could please sleep in their room, but they always assured me that nothing was going to harm me. When they shut the door, I'd lie in my room and the darkness would stretch toward me as if it were trying to swallow me up!

I'd shut my eyes to the menacing shadows and the moonlight reflected through my window while my heart pounded against the silence of the night. When I could no longer bear it, I'd hide under my covers and pray a desperate plea: "Jesus, where are you? I'm afraid. Please be with me!"

Going to bed was such a struggle every night that eventually my mom gave in and let me sleep with the lights on (mind you, this was a big deal for an immigrant mother bent on saving every penny on our electricity bill).

Several years later, due to a major financial disruption in our lives, our family moved into a small two-bedroom apartment in a new city. My sister and I had to share a room, and amidst the hardship of all the changes to our family life, something amazing happened. On the first night in our new home, with my sister asleep next to me, I was no longer afraid of the dark! I slept with relief, knowing I was no longer alone.

As a spiritual director, I recognize how many of us feel when we are in a spiritually disorienting, desperate place. When we are in spiritual crises, we call out and ask God, "Where are you? I'm afraid. Please be with me!" We feel vulnerable, abandoned, lost. The darkness of hopelessness stretches toward us as if to consume us.

Financial strain, relational fractures, the ongoing injustice of systemic prejudice, family dysfunction, academic struggles, and social pressure are all traumatic experiences that can contribute to these periods of darkness. We feel that God has left us and we are alone in our pain. Often Fours are particularly vulnerable to these feelings of isolation because of our sense that we are "different."

In Mark 4, the disciples have a similar experience of spiritual and physical disruption. They are traveling with Jesus across the Sea of Galilee when a sudden and turbulent storm comes upon them. The disciples fear for their lives and call to Jesus for help, but he remains asleep "on a cushion" (Mark 4:38). The disciples are flustered that Jesus is asleep, unbothered by the storm threatening to take their lives. They wake him and Jesus calms the wind and sea with complete authority.

Growing up, I was always bothered that Jesus was sleeping in this story. Why wasn't he awake when everyone needed him? However, over the years, I've grown to be comforted by Jesus' response in the storm. I've begun to see his response as an invitation for us to rest beside him. In the midst of seemingly uncontrollable, stormy circumstances, Jesus is still in full authority and will keep us safe. With this in mind, instead of resisting the dark, we can adjust our vision to see and find relief next to a resting Jesus.

Have you experienced a season of spiritual crisis or disorientation? What does it mean for you to see your pain, depression, fear, or isolation as a place where Jesus has not abandoned you but instead is inviting you to take rest next to him?

Take some time writing out an honest prayer of need and hope.

BEARING THE
IMAGE OF GOD

MY FOURNESS COMES IN HANDY as a parent—I am always planning creative activities and art projects for my kids. Last Halloween, instead of buying our costumes, I decided we were going to make our own. I took two huge pieces of butcher paper and cut out outlines of my children's bodies. I told them to draw a self-portrait of themselves as their costume. They loved the idea, and after grabbing a handful of markers, a rainbow of construction paper, and mismatched stickers, they began their masterpieces.

I was happy to see Ellie dive deep into her self-portrait project. She started by cutting out several blue buttons and a yellow hat. I encouraged her, telling her what a great job she was doing. I turned to see what progress my son had made.

When I looked back at Ellie, I was surprised to find that the two blue buttons she had cut out were placed horizontally on her face and the yellow that she had made was framing the entire face. I realized, in shock, that the blue buttons were not buttons; they were blue eyes, and her yellow hat was actually yellow hair.

I was so taken aback when I realized what she was doing that I did not know how to react. I tried to be casual, thinking maybe she had misunderstood my directions. I said, uneasily, "Oh, Ellie! You don't have blue eyes! You have beautiful dark brown eyes! And you don't have yellow hair! You have beautiful black hair!"

Then Ellie said something that sank my mama heart to the floor. "No, Umma! This is what I want to look like when I grow up!"

I said to her, "Oh, Ellie! When you get older, you're going to look like Umma—black hair and brown eyes! God made you so perfect!" I was trying to hold back tears.

Ellie just continued to say, "But this is what I want to look like when I get older."

In that moment I felt anger and sadness. I was reminded of my own growing-up years, when I internalized the belief that my Asianness wasn't good enough. I splashed chemicals on my hair to lighten the color, used tape and glue to try to make my eyelids bigger and rounder, not so "chinky," clipped my nose with a hairpin for hours to try to make the bridge sharper, and pushed against my cheekbones during class so my face wasn't so flat. It was a shock to acknowledge that, like me, Ellie had also internalized the notion that who she was, what she looked like—her Asianness—was not enough. In her drawing, she had erased herself.

The questions I had for Ellie were like a mirror I was holding up to myself. How could I help her love herself? What would it look like for Ellie to know her value and worth? Did she know how special she was? Didn't she know that she was made uniquely and perfectly to reflect the image of God?

While my journey is specific to my Korean American background, my questions about feeling flawed are common to the experience of a Four. I ask myself: "How can I grow in self-love? What would it look like for me to know my value and worth? Do I truly believe I am made uniquely and perfectly to reflect the image of God?"

One day Ellie will know for sure that she cannot change who God made her to be. As her Umma, I'll continue to show her how proud I am to be Asian—to tell her that she and I both are made in the image of God, wonderfully and fearfully made as Asian women—black hair, dark brown eyes, and all. Our cultural identity is worth embracing, our stories are worth telling—we are worth representing. She and I bear the image of God to one another and to the world.

Take some time to reflect and journal on the following statements as a practice of self-love: I love myself. I love who God made me to be. My skin tone, eyes, nose, height, hair—it wasn't a mistake. My race, my culture, my disability, my gender, my sexuality, my story—I uniquely reflect the image of God in the way only I can. I was created to fully stand in dignity and bear witness to God in this world.

Hear and receive God's loving words over you: "[You are] fearfully and wonderfully made" (Psalm 139:14).

CO-CREATING

FOR THE MAJORITY OF MY UPBRINGING, I lived a very compartmentalized faith. My faith was tied to a specific set of "spiritual activities," like going to church on Sundays or having "quiet time" in the mornings. My understanding of spirituality at the time was limited and limiting. I treated my spiritual life as though it were simply one piece among many in the pie chart of my life.

There was no space for my Fourness to exist in this version of spirituality. I believed my perceived flaws, the emotional complexity I carried, the ways I was drawn to beauty and art, and my desire for authentic connection were a distraction to seeking God. I did not grasp that God longed to reach into every nuance of who I was and that my "real life" could never be compartmentalized out of my spirituality.

When I was pregnant with my firstborn, Sammy, I felt uncomfortable with the word "pregnant," so I kept telling people that I was "with child." Anytime I felt someone's eyes drift to my belly, I would exclaim, "I am with child!" It was my way of claiming a new reality, that Sammy was a very real part of my life. My spouse, Dave, and I would explain to people over the next nine months that God was cocreating new life in us.

When we look through the Scriptures, our relationship with God is described as abiding in the vine, living in Christ, doing nothing apart from Jesus, walking in the Spirit, knowing the love of Christ beyond all knowledge, praying unceasingly, and doing all for the glory of God. The Bible gives us a vibrant, abundant vision for our spiritual lives. It essentially states that our spiritual life *is* life *with* God. Our relationship with God pours into any role, relationship, vocation, dream, community, and responsibility we have. In the same way I described myself as "with child" for those nine months, God is "with us"—and for more than a mere nine months. God is always with us, cocreating new life with us every moment of every day!

As a Four who initially understood spirituality as doing designated "holy" things for God or being in sacred places, I now see my spiritual life as "life with God"—every moment is an opportunity to cocreate and be *with* God. God cares for us, mothers us, and invites us toward life. This understanding has shifted the way I show up in this world in my Fourness and in my creative expression—God is no longer a task master but one who invites me into participation and collaboration. Even as I write this reflection, I believe God's Spirit is cowriting with me!

What are the ways you tend to compartmentalize your spirituality from everyday life? How does the idea of cocreating encourage you toward a deeper spiritual integration of your work and being?

If this concept is new to you, try practicing being in the presence of God. Practice becoming mindful of Jesus throughout the day, believing that he is available to you and with you, no matter where you are or what mundane or magnificent task you're taking part in.

BLESSING

EVERY YEAR, KOREANS GATHER with extended family to celebrate New Year's Day. The day is usually filled with activity. The women are frantically busy in the kitchen, steam hissing out of big pots full of broth, ready for the addition of rice cakes and dumplings. Excited children run around in their colorful *hanboks*, or traditional Korean attire, the sounds of the Rose Bowl Parade blaring from the television.

Depending on the family, there is an order to the day's events, the most important being the ceremony of bowing to the elders and receiving a New Year's blessing. This ceremony is a tradition that has been observed and passed down for thousands of years.

The bow that we practice during this ceremony is called *seh-beh*. It requires us to kneel to the floor and place our hands on the ground, with our faces almost touching the floor. This year, my parents, who are in their early sixties, bowed to our family's oldest living elders—my great-uncle and great-aunt, who are in their late eighties. As they stayed bowing, my uncle and aunt shared words of blessing and life: "We love you. We're so proud of you. You are raising your kids well and you are faithful to our God. Look at how much you've done with your lives this year. Although there have been many financial struggles and difficult circumstances, we believe in you. God will help you through it all. We love you."

I have always loved this day of blessing. To be seen and affirmed speaks deeply to my number Four soul! During our *seh-beh*, we are required to receive the blessing. We cannot reject or resist it. We simply receive it, even if it feels uncomfortable or unwarranted and we feel undeserving. It is a cultural tradition that reminds me of the ways we respond to God's words of life and blessing over us.

Within all of us, and especially within Fours, there is a deep longing to be seen, known, and believed in. However, many of us think God's blessing cannot come to us. Our actions reflect a belief that in order to be blessed, we must earn it. We feel we need to be holier or better than we are to receive this blessing. Some of us carry wounds on our souls, scars originating in memories of betrayal, abandonment, rejection, and internalized oppression that manifest as scarcity, pain, worthlessness, or rejection of self and others. We don't have the capacity to imagine that God would want to bless someone like us.

But from the beginning of creation, God creates and blesses humanity by calling it "very good" (Genesis 1:31).

Throughout the Old Testament God's people are called into blessing and called out to bless all nations. In the New Testament God speaks blessing over Jesus: "You are my Son, whom I love; with you I am well pleased" (Mark 1:11). Throughout the Gospels Jesus' life models to us power laid down for the liberation of all of humanity: "Freely you have received; freely give" (Matthew 10:8). You've been blessed—now let this blessing overflow to others.

Even if we try to resist or reject God's blessing, we discover there is nothing we can do to remove it from us. God's blessing is free. It is an act of grace. God chooses us as an act of grace. God takes pride in us and loves us as an act of grace. God sees, hears, and knows us as an act of grace. We don't have to wait until New Year's Day to receive God's blessing. We can receive it any moment of any day. We simply allow God to see us, know us, and believe in us. No fixing, hiding, diminishing, or striving. We are loved just as we are.

This blessing doesn't stop with us. God blesses us so we can become people of blessing in a time when cursing, oppression, and dehumanization are normalized and emboldened. In the name of Jesus, we follow the *way* of Jesus. We commit to speaking truth to power, cultivating life, bringing hope, carrying peace, seeking justice, liberating the oppressed, embodying compassion, and loving with the unconditional love that we've received.

Take some time to read Numbers 6:24-26:

> The LORD bless you
> and keep you;
> the LORD make his face shine on you
> and be gracious to you;
> the LORD turn his face toward you
> and give you peace.

Read it two to three times, allowing these words to wash over you. What words or phrases stand out to you? How might you receive God's blessing today? What are some ways you can be a person of overflowing blessing for others today?

BOUNDARIES

DURING MY SENIOR YEAR of high school I was voted "Friendliest" by my class. In my yearbook I share a picture with Arash Ghafari (the other "Friendliest"), both of us smiling and giving a thumbs-up. Being a friend always came naturally to me, and friendship was a measure of my worth in people's lives.

However, the flip side to being the "Friendliest" was that I functioned in a way that caused me deep anxiety and stress. I found my identity in showing up when I was needed. I would drop everything to be there for a friend. The thing is, I didn't want to be just one of the friends among friends. I wanted to be the friend who was the *best friend* to all my friends.

Eventually this need for validation and affirmation was exhausting and unsustainable, especially when I became a mom and eventually a pastor. There was no way to continue to extend myself in the same way I'd been doing. But as a Four, I wanted to be the most special, the one who outshone and outdid others.

I know, I know—it sounds like I had some major issues with codependency and performance (which are both things

I've been working through during the past seven years in therapy). Part of my work with my therapist has been realizing my own history of struggling to create boundaries for myself.

This year I lost a friendship that broke me. I still don't know what I did wrong or why the friendship fell apart, but for some reason, the friend abruptly stopped returning my calls or seeking time together. . . . For days upon days, I would comb through each scenario we had shared and wonder, *What did I do wrong? Did I say something offensive? Maybe the friend of a friend said something about me that makes her think I'm a bad person. Why won't she just tell me instead of ignoring my calls?*

I tried to talk to her a few times, but she said nothing was wrong and continued to distance herself. I started making up wild delusions about why she chose to leave our friendship.

My anxiety about the situation eventually took over dinner conversations, car rides, and pillow talks with my spouse, Dave. Finally, exasperated by my inability to move on, Dave exclaimed, "Why would you want to be friends with someone who obviously doesn't want to be friends with you?"

I was defensive and annoyed with Dave. He was speaking truthful words, but the anxiety and shame I had been suppressing came pouring out through tears. I knew he was right—I needed to take care of myself. I needed to create a boundary for myself—to stop giving away my power only to be rejected and hurt. I needed to move on from the stinging pain of rejection—but I wasn't sure how.

I recently visited my two dear friends Beans and Sami for our monthly spam musubi exchange. As we ate together, I admired the greenery around their home, commenting on the fiddle-leaf fig trees that had grown substantially since the last time I had visited. In response, Sami shared that these trees grow according to the size of the pot they've been planted in—meaning they have the capacity to get larger if their roots are placed in new soil with room to expand. As she shared this, I realized God was giving me an analogy for friendship.

Although we may not recognize it when it's happening, sometimes we outgrow relationships, and sometimes relationships outgrow us. I still don't have answers as to why my friendship broke apart, but I am learning to accept it.

As a Four, I can put too much stake in my emotions, and this situation has pushed me to evaluate where I find my worth. I have had to lean on God, my soul friends, and Dave, who have spoken truth to me over and over again. And even though any reminder of this friendship still stings when it enters my thoughts, I've decided to make room for new soil without this friendship. To let go, to allow myself to heal, and to no longer hold onto roots that aren't holding onto me. To refuse to see myself as a mistake or a burden but to realize that sometimes we just need fresh soil and a new pot.

What do boundaries in relationships look like for you?
Are you in a season of letting go of friendships and
cultivating new ones? If, like me, you are in a season of
grieving lost friendships, allow God to minister to you
and hold your tears. You are not a burden and you are
not a mistake. You are beloved and worthy.

YOU ARE WELCOME

MY MOM DID NOT KNOW my dad very long before she decided to marry him. She was a young nursing student, naive and desperate to escape poverty. My dad's immediate family had decided to immigrate to America for a better life, and that was his promise to her when he proposed. My mom left her entire family to be with my dad, trusting that he would take care of her in a foreign country. My dad intended to keep his promise, looking forward to his piece of the American dream.

As my parents built their life and made their home in America, they found early on that as immigrants, as "foreigners," they were not welcome. I have distinct memories of my dad, who worked in a gas station, regularly being spoken down to because of what he looked like. My mom was mocked at my school by other parents because of her thick Korean accent. It felt like everywhere we went, people treated my parents as less-than or as a burden to have to deal with. Sometimes we would hear a voice randomly shout out to us, "Go back where you came from! Go back to your country! Go home!"

Fours tend to abandon environments that bring shame or rejection. And in those years, I had such a desperate longing to belong. In my immaturity, shame, and insecurity, I wished I wasn't associated with my parents, and for years I would do all I could to distance myself from anything that would cause me to be perceived as too foreign or different from whiteness. These moments were the beginning of many more like it—a reckoning of my identity, the erasing of my heritage and culture.

For people of color, memories like these are shared experiences. Experiencing racial trauma time and time again results in a sense that our existence is not enough. Although my Korean identity and heritage were the truest parts of me, my need to belong motivated a betrayal of my roots, my story, and my identity.

Have you been "othered" or shamed for your identity? Fours often experience shame for our inner complexity and emotional intensity. We feel misunderstood as outsiders and inferior for our perceived insignificance. For people of color who identify as Fours, we internalize a multi-layered narrative that we were born missing something inside that makes us fundamentally flawed, and yet we yearn to find safe places that allow us to be our true selves.

Lately I've been thinking about Jesus' piercing words in Matthew 25:43: "I was a stranger and you did not invite me in." I've been interchanging the word "stranger" with "foreigner." He goes on to say, "Whatever you did not do for one of the least of these, you did not do for me" (Matthew 25:45). Jesus identifies as one who was othered, misunderstood, and mistreated. He dignifies the experiences of the stranger and foreigner, and if I could go back to my younger self, I would tell her, "Jesus welcomes you, just as you are."

Jesus and his parents were a refugee family who fled their hometown due to government-sanctioned violence. Jesus had "no place to lay his head" (Luke 9:58) as a peasant Palestinian teacher who was pushed to the margins of society. As one who was homeless, Jesus welcomes the refugee, the foreigner, the expendable, and the vulnerable. He welcomes the woman, the immigrant, the wounded, the unclean, and the weary. He welcomes the outcast of society, the demon-possessed, and the unredeemable. He welcomes across lines of race, sexuality, and gender and says, "Come to me, all you who are weary, and I will give you rest" (Matthew 11:28).

> Take some time to imagine Jesus saying these words to you: "Come to me if you're weary, if you've been rejected, othered, or humiliated, and I will give you rest." Allow yourself to rest in his presence. What do you feel? What do you need to say? What are you longing to hear Jesus say to you?

I'M GOING TO BE A SINGER!

MY FRIEND GRACE recently asked me what I wanted to be when I was little. I laughed as I reminisced about my childhood and my flashy, flamboyant self. Growing up, I had boldly declared to anyone who was around, "I'm going to be a singer!"

I come from a generation of singers. My proud grandmother would always sing so loudly in the church choir that I cringed in my seat; her alto became even louder during the chorus. My father regularly serenaded my mother in the evenings, his baritone lifting up the Korean folk songs that reminded them of their lives in South Korea. His eyes would close and sometimes tear as he left our living room for another place in his past. Music had magical powers! I grew up believing that my voice could touch lives and change the world.

However, as I grew older, this dream gradually faded. I was a daughter of immigrants, and my parents' expectations were clear: good grades, approved extracurricular activities, and a financial contribution to the family by working two jobs after school. At church, I was involved in a plethora of ministry opportunities while internalizing a disapproval of vocal females. As an Asian American woman, I absorbed the cultural expectations of meekness and service. In trying to please everyone else while navigating my survival in dominant-majority environments, I lost my purpose and ability to dream along the way. As a Four, I was overwhelmed and confused by my paradoxical desire to fit into societal expectations yet break away to become someone unique.

Something unexpected happened when I began pastoring about four years ago. I began to use my voice in a way I could never have fathomed. I was using my voice not only to sing but also to preach, lead, and boldly speak truth to power. The yearning that had burned within me as a child was free. My voice was liberated from the confines of societal and cultural expectations. I was finally able to embrace the burning fire within me—a continuous flame that grounds me, inspires me, and pushes me toward creative expressions of hope and resilience.

As you look back at your childhood, what was it you hoped to become? How do you think your childhood dream relates to your Enneagram number? If you are a Four, what are the ways you are living into your authentic, unbound, and creative expression?

A SOUL FRIEND

I MET MY BEST FRIEND, Tiffany, during my first year of college. We were in the same residential hall but on different floors in the off-white, all-girls' building. It didn't take long before she and I became good friends, sharing a penchant for hunting down fast food past midnight and laughing until our stomachs hurt. We also shared an intense devotion to intramural tennis and, most significantly, an unspoken value for authentic connection. I didn't know it back then, but meeting Tiff and gaining her friendship would become one of the most transformative experiences of my life.

Tiff was confident, fun, assertive, gracious, and charming. She was fearless in speaking her mind, advocating for others, and pursuing her dreams. But she also embodied fearless vulnerability, inviting others into honest connection and self-reflection. Tiff not only pushed the typical threshold of acceptable disclosure well beyond its limits but also welcomed it with open arms. She was a free spirit who didn't need anyone's approval, yet she created space for everyone around her to belong.

Prior to our friendship, I wasn't comfortable with the emotional complexity I carried around as a Four. My emotional needs were so vast, varied, and mysterious—even to myself! Like many Fours, I often felt the need to hide parts of myself in order to be accepted. I had been told over the course of my life that I was "too much" and therefore internalized an undercurrent of abandonment.

When Tiff came into my life, her consistency, genuine care, and curiosity modeled an acceptance that seeped its way into my spirit, eventually leading to my own self-acceptance. Tiff was unafraid of my emotional intensity. In fact, she validated the very complexities I tried to diminish. Every conversation was a new layer to uncover, a galaxy of insights to untangle, and her self-awareness and emotional maturity gave me the courage to embrace my own self. On any given day or night, we could process anything on any given subject. Tiff masterfully held my inner contradictions and motivations in tension with me—no judgment, no rejection, no expectation for change. She genuinely sought to understand.

We didn't have Enneagram language at the time, but the reason this friendship was so special is that we had found Fourness in each other. Through our friendship, God was bringing healing—a place to belong, a place to be understood, a place to simply be. We were kindred spirits, true soul friends.

The last ten years Tiff and I have been far apart from each other—she and her family now live in Belgium, and my family is still in California. We've taken paths that no longer overlap as easily as they did in college, and though we grieve that our families don't get to see each other day to day, the core of our friendship is always there.

For seventeen years, no topic of conversation has been off the table. The longevity of friendship has given us a unique perspective in knowing the historical truth of each other's life choices, circumstances, and experiences. We strive to understand and we hold space. We trust each other enough to disagree with no agenda for change, yet we still seek to empathize and embody compassion. We call each other to the truest, most whole version of who God has made us to be for ourselves and for others: a soul friend.

If you are a Four, think back to a time you felt deeply understood. What healing came from that encounter? What qualities in a friendship mean the most to you as a Four? Write them down. What relationships in your life have helped you to embrace your emotional complexity and depth more fully?

JUST EYES

THE FIRST TIME MY FAMILY enjoyed Disneyland together as a family of four, Sammy was almost three years old and Ellie was not quite one. The magic of Disneyland descended upon us the moment we passed the ticket booth. We were entranced by the smell of sugary churros and toasted pretzels as Mickey and Minnie waved at us from the corner. Main Street was a bustle of activity, storefronts enticing us with toys and candy, musical entertainers serenading us, horses and trolleys traversing the road.

From the moment we entered the park, I was determined to capture every special moment on my phone. I recorded all of Sammy's reactions—character meet-and-greets, his opinion on the ride he had just disembarked from, his wide grin after tasting his first churro. I had Sammy pose with statues and buildings, and of course, we couldn't miss a family photo in front of the iconic Sleeping Beauty castle!

Around 2 p.m., my daughter was long overdue for her afternoon nap, so my spouse strolled with her toward a quieter area. I decided it was the perfect time to take Sammy on my favorite childhood ride: Dumbo! We walked over and waited in line for our turn. I took out my phone, as I had done throughout the day, and began to interview my son about his Disney experience so far. He exhaustedly obliged.

It was finally time for us to get on the ride. Once we were buckled up, I took out my phone again to capture Samuel's first Dumbo experience. As I was getting ready to take footage, I felt a pull on my sleeve. Sammy looked up at me and pleaded, "Umma, Umma, no phone . . . no phone . . . just eyes."

I was so taken aback by his request that I needed a moment to understand what he meant. Sammy was asking me to see him, asking me to be present, asking me to be there *with* him.

As a Four, this story encompasses my struggle with being fully present. It's not necessarily that I'm distracted by the physical happenings around me; it's that I am perpetually in a state of either reliving the past or daydreaming about the future. In this particular case, my futuristic concern with preserving my kids' Disneyland memories interfered with my ability to be present with Sammy. I was not fully where I needed to be.

If the concept of FOMO (fear of missing out) describes a phenomenon of social media–induced pressures, Fours have FOMO about the expectations of our past and the pressures of our future. Our FOMO tells us we're always about to miss something or just missed something. We lose track of the present moment because we are paying attention to what happened, what could have happened, or what could still happen. We get lost in the details of our past or run ahead of ourselves into a future not guaranteed.

Don't get me wrong—this past-future ability is a unique Four superpower. It makes us incredibly reflective while undergirding our ability to dream. However, if we don't regularly examine this tendency, we forget to live the life right in front of us. When I indulge myself in past-future living, I can carry unhealthy levels of anxiety that drive rash or impulsive decisions. There have been seasons when I have let this anxiety run unchecked and projected unwarranted frustration, stress, and insecure behavior onto the people closest to me.

As I've matured in self-awareness, I've had to incorporate the discipline of having "just eyes." This means that I meet regularly with a spiritual director who helps parse my anxiety from reality. In my rule of life, I have specific hours scheduled throughout the week to dream about the future and reflect on the past. Without these rhythms, I can get lost in myself. And I never want to lose the magnitude and implications of this truth: my real life has not already been lived, and it is not going to be lived sometime in the future.

My real life is happening right now, right in front of me.

If you are a Four, do you have a tendency to relive your past or fantasize about your future? What practices or rhythms have you incorporated in order to live fully in the present? How can you create space for yourself to reflect or dream without interfering with your real life in front of you?

NO COMPARISONS

GROWING UP, I ALWAYS compared myself to my sister—it seemed like she could do anything she put her mind to. She was freakishly talented at many things, and I wanted to be just like her. To her annoyance, I copied everything she did. Play the piano? Me too! Play tennis? Me too! Get a perm? Me too!

As high schoolers, we began to compete with one another in sports. We would duke it out on the tennis court, and the "loser" would have to walk home while the winner drove. One day we dared each other to run twenty blocks from the ocean pier to our apartment. My sister, who had been recovering from an injury, couldn't finish, but I showed no mercy. I felt only the soaring elation of finishing the race (and beating my sister)!

Comparison saturates the way we understand ourselves. We look around us to see where we fit in or if what we have is enough. We feel the weight of comparison throughout our lives—contrasting ourselves to our siblings, peers at school, colleagues at work, and even random strangers we encounter.

Social media adds an explosiveness to our inclination to compare. It feeds us a barrage of images and narratives every day—a picture-perfect reel of photos, flawlessly edited, posted with intent—that tell us we are or aren't enough or how #blessed we are. Even though many of us know these images uphold unrealistic and distorted standards of normativity, we still allow them to trickle into our individual thinking, our institutions, our organizations, and the very systems we are part of.

Over the years I've tried to pay greater attention to how my envy and comparison shows up in my Fourness. Comparison often creates a barrier that prevents me from seeing another person as a deeply loved child of God. When I go down the path of envy, I begin to internalize that there is room for only one to be at the proverbial "top" instead of seeing others as fellow companions on the journey of life and faith.

The message of Jesus is that there is room for all in the kingdom of God. Every single person, crafted and molded with purpose, love, and life, exists to bear the image of God in the way only they can. There is no scarcity in God's kingdom, only abundance. God does not compare us, and God's love never runs out for any of us—it is a reservoir that keeps on giving, unconditionally and extravagantly.

Because Fours live in the Heart/Feeling Triad, we often forget to be in our bodies. Embodied practices help us discipline ourselves away from feelings of envy and comparison, and toward being present with our own unique selves before God.

I often engage in a specific embodied practice to deal with my comparison tendencies: I open up my hands. Any time I feel "clenched fists" or scarcity toward someone, I ask God to give me open hands. Opening my hands is a way to confess and release my inclination to compare. It is my way of surrendering my bitterness, envy, resentment of others, and rejection of my true self as God's beloved. It is my way of saying to God, *My heart is open to your love. As I give you my selfishness, hatred, and jealousy, would you fill me with your compassion and grace in order to see your child(ren) as the imago Dei? Help me also to have compassion for myself. To love myself as you love me. Amen.*

Throughout the week, practice moving from clenched fists to open hands wherever you are—in line at the grocery store, as you review a colleague's creative work, during a tense conversation with your partner, in traffic during rush hour. Notice how this practice creates an embodied movement for transformation. With open hands, you actively claim your belovedness and the belovedness of others. In this posture, you are a carrier and reservoir of God's grace.

NO SUBSTITUTIONS

AT ONE POINT DURING a busy and harried season of life, I tried a number of approaches to increased self-care: watching TV after putting the kids down, indulging myself with treats I wouldn't normally have, hanging out more often with friends, reading enjoyable books, adding fun activities to my plate, and so on . . . but these things didn't fill me up! They were temporary, momentary reliefs from the stress and anxiety I was holding, but the relief and rest did not last.

This is the difference between self-care and soul care.

Only God can fill me up at the soul level. Only God can renew me, remind me of my worth and value, speak life into what is dead in my life, and help me discern the right decision or path to take. Only God's words can comfort me and heal my wounds; only God can remind me of my identity as the beloved. It is only God's presence that can overflow to the people I love, the individuals I shepherd, and the work I've been called to do.

Carving out time for soul care is one of the greatest battles I will fight throughout my life. My Fourness will have me talking in circles about my need to spend time with God instead of actually taking action. And then my Three wing will shout at me to "Be productive!" or question, "What will spending time in solitude do for you? There are a million things to get done! No time to waste!"

But Jesus talked about soul care, made time for it, and did it. He retreated and modeled to us a rhythm of getting away to be refreshed in the presence of God so that he could, with integrity, do the work of God. His intimate relationship with God was the source of his power, compassion, and wisdom. In his example and through his words, Jesus invites us to join him in this same place of renewal.

I am claiming this truth over and over again in my life: There is no substitute for the presence of God.

Imagine Jesus saying to you, "Come away with me to a quiet place and rest awhile." Read these words slowly and meditatively three more times. As you read, take notice of what words stand out to you. Write down your reflections, whether you feel resistance or relief in these words.

How can you take action to further your authentic connection with God? What is one way you can get away this week for the sole intent of spending time with God? Mark it in your calendar and stick to it.

WHERE IS YOUR BROTHER?

IN THE BEGINNING CHAPTERS of Genesis, we are confronted with humanity's first murder. Cain, the firstborn son of Adam and Eve, kills his younger brother Abel in a jealous rage. When God asks Cain where his brother is, Cain responds, "I don't know. . . . Am I my brother's keeper?" (Genesis 4:9).

Last summer one of my mentors led a group from our church on an Asian American civil rights pilgrimage. During this trip we remembered and lamented a civil liberties failure in our American history seventy-eight years ago, when President Roosevelt signed Executive Order 9066, a policy that resulted in nearly 120,000 innocent Japanese-American citizens, immigrants, and nationals being forced out of their homes, businesses, and neighborhoods to live in camps with prison-like conditions.

Across the West Coast, families and individuals were given seven days to report to their respective camps. They were ordered to bring only what they could carry—for some, that was their baby or child; for others, it was a few items of clothing, bedding, and cookware.

In Arcadia, California, ten minutes from where I live, Japanese Americans were sent to the Santa Anita racetrack, where children, parents, individuals, and families were boarded in horse stalls that stunk of manure, mud, and filth. These "assembly centers" were a grim foreshadowing of the dehumanizing camp conditions that were to come for Japanese Americans. Over the course of World War II, between 1942 and 1945, every Japanese American was tagged with an ID number and sent to one of ten concentration camps across the nation. Families were separated; many did not know if they would ever see their aunts, uncles, mothers, fathers, grandparents, brothers, sisters, or children ever again.

As a Four, I used to think that empathy alone was the work of justice. After hearing a story of injustice and letting it break my heart, I didn't think there was any power within me to make change. Over time, I realized that it's not enough to *feel*—we need to *do*.

We visited Manzanar, the first concentration camp and the one that would eventually become a blueprint for others. We saw firsthand the horrific conditions meant to strip Japanese Americans of their human dignity, supposedly to "protect Americans" from Japanese spies. Widespread narratives stemming from racial prejudice perpetuated the dehumanization of innocent Japanese Americans and were used to justify government-sanctioned oppression. In total, close to two thousand people died at these camps. On our final stop, we visited the cemetery that bore the bodies of a hundred and fifty children, women, and men. The grief was so deep from the heaviness of these unjust deaths that it was hard to breathe at times.

Today, the same weaponized rhetoric embedded with fear and hate is being used to marginalize and divide. We are seeing our government separate children from their families at the border, state-sanctioned brutality and abuse against Black and Brown communities, deliberative systemic oppression of immigrants of color, and the displacement of refugees—a striking pattern of dehumanization grounded in white supremacy. These acts of violence against humanity demand a response from the church. Are we, like Cain, turning our ears and eyes away from these injustices, asking, "Am I my brother's keeper?" Or are we hearing the weeping voice of God crying out to each of us, "Listen! Your brother's blood cries out to me from the ground" (Genesis 4:10).

As Fours, we must take our gift of empathy and allow it to transform into action and resistance—whether through creating, protesting, offering a sacred space, marching, speaking out, or organizing. More and more I am realizing how easy it has been for me to sit back and allow others to take charge because I feel "too flawed" or emotionally overwhelmed to make any real change. However, I am taking cues from what healthy Ones embody in discipline, principle, and consistency. These qualities also live in my Fourness as I move into integration. When Fours find our significance in justice, a new fire will burn within us to change the world.

> What comes up within you as you hear the question God asks Cain: "Where is your brother?" (Genesis 4:9). What issues of justice are you proximate to? If you are a Four, how can you seek to move beyond empathy and take tangible steps toward action?

HOME IN MY BODY

MY PARENTS WERE IN THE hospitality business for almost twenty years. This meant I worked at their restaurant every summer in high school and college.

I was a terrible waitress. I lost and mixed up orders, sent the wrong orders to the kitchen, delivered the wrong orders to tables. It got so bad that my mother finally demoted me from waitress to busboy—I cleaned tables and washed dishes away from any contact with customers.

I wish I could say my substandard waitressing skills were specific to my time at the restaurant, but for as long as I can remember, I've struggled to be totally present wherever I am physically. In other words, I'm often not at home in my body.

When I began studying the Enneagram, my teachers taught me that Twos, Threes, and Fours live in the Heart (Feeling) Triad. For those new to this concept, triads teach us about our habitual responses, and every number belongs to one of three: Heart (Feeling), Head (Fear), or Gut (Anger). As someone in the Heart Triad, I process my experiences by way of emotion and feeling. We yearn for meaningful experiences with others where we feel deep connection and purpose, but we tend to neglect connection to our heads and bodies.

I've come to realize, however, that this tendency to detach from my body is also a result of my upbringing. Like many who grew up in the church, I was taught that our bodies were untrustworthy guides—especially women's bodies, which were deemed a source of temptation to men. In church we often talked about the need to "die to the flesh" in ways that left no room for an embodied theology. We didn't have a framework to grasp what trauma scholar Resmaa Menaken says in his book *My Grandmother's Hands*: "The body, not the thinking brain, is . . . where we process most of what happens to us. It is also where we do most of our healing, including our emotional and psychological healing." The experiences we incur—our pleasures, joys, pain, and traumas—are lived out and carried in our bodies.

I've been trying to integrate a spirituality that honors and dignifies my body. When I think of an embodied theology, I look at Jesus' life and see that his incarnation is a guide for how we are to esteem our bodies. My dear friend Arielle, a powerful spoken word artist, often talks about coming home to our bodies, and I am working toward that. My body is not simply a mask to cover what's going on inside of me. My body holds the fruit and the loss of my life experiences, both the beauty and brutality. And even though as a Four the journey to embodied living is a lifelong effort, I am grateful to be on the path of becoming whole.

For the past six years or so, I have been practicing an embodied ritual every morning. When I wake up (before my kids run into my room), I lie on my back and slowly breathe in and out. I pay attention to my inhale and exhale. I do it several times as I position my arms and hands so that they are upward-facing but still resting on the bed. In this vulnerable posture of openness and surrender, I try to pay attention to what's happening in my body.

If anxiety begins to creep up (which it does, every day), I hold the anxious thought or feeling graciously and without condemning myself, imagining it dissolving in God's presence. I begin to speak with God's Spirit within me: "I'm open to you today. I'm open. I'm not closed off. Be with me—help me to love you with all my mind, heart, body, and soul. I am yours."

Sometimes I incorporate a breath prayer and place my hands on my stomach and heart, inhaling, "Mother God," and exhaling, "Heal me" or "Heal our world." Throughout the day I practice paying attention to my breathing, and on especially hard days I hug my body and thank her for being with me, carrying me, sustaining me throughout the day.

Take time to intentionally engage in one of the practices described at the end of this day's reading, and reflect on the experience afterward. What does it mean for you to come home to your body?

HAN AND BEARING PAIN

ONE HOT SUMMER DAY I was working in my parents' restaurant when an elderly Korean couple walked in. I greeted them from behind the counter: "*Uh-suh-oh-sae yo*," meaning, "Welcome to our restaurant." As I approached with water and menus, the man became agitated. He was furious and shouted at me in Korean, "How dare you wear that?"

That day I'd casually worn a shirt with a vibrant image of a red sun with rays shooting out. Although the shirt had no special meaning to me, the graphic triggered violent memories of torture and abuse for this Korean elder. From 1910 to 1945, Japan's rising sun war flag was a symbol of its brutal occupation and colonization of Korea. Koreans were stripped of their language, their heritage, their culture, and even their very names. Nearly 725,000 Koreans were forced to work in Japan and its colonies, and hundreds of thousands of "comfort" women were forced into sexual slavery in Japanese military brothels.

In my initial interaction with the elderly couple, I thought I was the victim in this story. As a Four, I have a tendency to take things personally, and I felt that the Korean man's tears and anger toward me were misdirected. Here I was, trying to extend hospitality and kindness, but I was attacked!

I used to wonder why Koreans couldn't just move on. The war was more than fifty years ago—why hold on to this bitterness, anger, and sorrow? But this was an ignorant and privileged way of thinking. As a Four, I was projecting an individualized and approximate approach onto my community of elders.

In my ignorance, I had hurt this man deeply. There is a word in Korean, *han*, that is difficult to fully translate in English. *Han* encompasses the painful tearing apart of one's heart due to injustice and oppression. It describes both a collective and individual experience of suffering that comes from unjust political and social systems. Theologian Grace Ji-Sun Kim, in her book *The Holy Spirit: Hand-Raisers, Han, and the Holy Ghost,* articulates that if *han* isn't released in a positive way, it can bring destruction, death, and violence into one's life or community. *Han* needs to be set free in order for healing to take place, for one to become whole again.

Koreans who survived Japanese colonization still carry this pain and suffering. Their *han* has not been fully healed, and a lack of formal apology for the atrocities committed against them by the Japanese government exacerbates their pain. Their collective *han* has not been set free.

When someone else expresses pain, it is easy for us to make it about ourselves. And when we see the suffering of others, it is often easier to turn away. Carrying someone's anguish and sadness alongside them requires responsibility. It requires work. It requires that we listen. It requires an open heart. It requires a willingness to be changed by someone's story of suffering, their *han*.

Integrated Fours are deeply present to others' suffering. When we function from our true self, our emotional depth and intuitiveness allow us to show up with compassion and empathy. The ability to bear pain is one of the unique gifts of a Four.

In the Gospels, we see Jesus invite all to his table of solidarity, vulnerability, hospitality, and hope. When we join his table of expansive love, we find that those who were once strangers have become fellow brothers and sisters in our shared humanity. Ultimately, we discover that in seeking the welfare of others, we in turn find our own.

One of the most powerful passages in Scripture is "Jesus wept" (John 11:35). Jesus' compassion overtakes him as he enters into the pain of Lazarus's death. In a similar way, what would it look like for you to "mourn with those who mourn" (Romans 12:15) and move toward the messiness of entering into a community's pain?

How can you work toward dismantling systems that cause *han* and brokenness in many communities?

TRUE REPENTANCE

THERE IS A SCENE IN THE MOVIE *Wall-E* where robots are defying the commands of the spaceship, and the loud-speakers repeat, "Rogue robots," "Rogue robots," "Rogue robots" over and over. After watching it, five-year-old Sammy asked, "Umma, what does 'rogue' mean?"

I tried to explain. "It means going your own way, kind of being wild, a little out of control from what you're supposed to be doing."

As a Four, I often justify my harmful behavior toward someone with the simple excuse, "I didn't mean to!" However, I am realizing the difference between intent and impact. Just because I didn't intend to hurt someone doesn't mean the impact of the harm was any less. I need to seek repentance, even if, according to me, my motivation was justifiable.

When I first became a follower of Jesus, I misunderstood the role of repentance in my life. I thought repentance was a once-in-a-lifetime thing. I thought becoming a Christian meant you repented one time, accepted Jesus as your Savior, and that was it—salvation achieved. But the longer I follow the way of Christ, the greater is my understanding that repentance is ongoing and lifelong. Our spiritual journey entails small conversions every single day.

When someone tells me I've hurt them or caused them harm, I'm learning to face a new direction of grace. This means I look outward rather than inward. Instead of taking personal offense or making excuses for my behavior, I strive to embody a repentance that lets my guard down, refuses to make it about me, and employs humility.

For me, repentance is inextricably connected to grace. Grace is always available to us even when we go "rogue." When we repent, we taste "the kingdom of God at hand"—Jesus restores us to God's family over and over again, as often as we need it.

What has repentance looked like in your faith tradition? Do you see repentance as an avenue for guilt and shame or a pathway to grace?

What are some of your tendencies or patterns in terms of "going rogue"?

Take some time to reflect on ways you may have justified harmful behavior toward your neighbor or God this past week. Write an honest prayer of repentance and seek where God may be inviting you to make amends.

SANCTUARY

AFTER TRANSITIONING OUT OF a church community I deeply loved, I found myself in the midst of a faith crisis—wondering who I was, what I was about, and where I was headed. For a while, church as I knew it felt foreign and hollow—worship songs felt distant and unrelatable, community felt forced and exhausting, the Scriptures seemed numb and deaf to my confusion and sorrow. As a Four whose core value system thrives on authenticity and genuine engagement, I was shaken up. My sense of disorientation was palpable, and no matter what I did, I couldn't find relief.

About six months after my decision to leave the church, my spouse unexpectedly planned a family camping trip to Yosemite. It would be a change of scene, a change of pace, a chance for us to simply be together. As a self-declared homebody, I passively tagged along.

When we arrived at our destination, my indifference ran smack into the unexpected activity of God. As we walked into the woods, the sanctuary of God opened up to me, sacred wonder hidden in every corner. I was invited into creation's liturgy—in the tender bubbling creek waters, the worshipful morning song of the blue jay, the exhale of peace in the rustling leaves, the motherly outstretched forest branches providing shade and relief, the piercing silence of Presence among the magnificent mountain peaks. The dependability of the sun's rising and setting, and its healing warmth, regenerated hope in my weary and tattered soul.

The beauty of creation all around me was revealing that God had been with me all along. As a Four, I needed to realize this. My loss of church community, wrestling with doubt, and lack of faithful inspiration weren't signs of failure or deficiency—they were another dimension of authentically engaging God.

In the midst of my grieving and aching, the playful mystery of nature breathed joy and life into me. As I encountered unpredictable trails and pathways, God's voice of love comforted me for the road ahead—"I am still breathing life into this world. . . . Breathe in, breathe out. . . . Come a little further down this path. . . . I'll be with you. . . . I'm with you." Loud voices of criticism, shame, and despair I'd been carrying around with me for weeks were silenced in the crunch of pine cones and dirt. The winds whispered a new song for me to hear: "You are my beloved. . . . I'm so proud of you." And the Voice deepest within assured me, "As sure as the sun rises, I am making all things new. As sure as the sun rises, there is still hope."

What are some recent ways you've experienced God
tending to your soul? If you find yourself in a season of
spiritual disorientation, how might a change of scenery
help you stay connected to God? Where in your real-life
circumstances can you seek an invitation toward
sacred wonder?

MARRIED TO A NINE

I AM MARRIED TO A NINE.

Dave and I met on a college missions trip to Panama, and what started as a fun and exciting friendship turned into a full-blown relationship over the course of the year. Early on when my friends would ask what drew me to Dave, I remember saying emphatically that my heart felt safe with him. It sounds cheesy, I know—but for me, feeling safe meant so much. As a Four, I did not have many places where I could be my full self and feel safe. My Fourness was complicated, messy, and overwhelming at times for the people in my life. But Dave not only accepted me as I was—he reveled in these multilayered aspects of my personality.

As a Nine, Dave did not romanticize who I was. He was allergic to inauthenticity. He had no pretense or ego about himself—he was steady, wise, genuine, stable, confident, funny, generous, and comfortable to be around. He was who he was—not more, not less—and this was incredibly refreshing to me as someone who constantly tried to prove I could be more or less if it brought me more belonging.

I now realize that my early perception of feeling "safe" with Dave wasn't all that special! Dave made everyone feel safe. Nines have a presence that is powerfully grounding. The more time I spent with Dave, the more I felt I was breathing in the very qualities he embodied. The more I got to know him, the more my trust and admiration grew.

We've now been together for thirteen years. Even though he doesn't share my emotional vigor or I his steady confidence, we've grown into each other. This is the stuff of marriage. We work toward growth and understanding, make space for honest connection, and provide a mirror of faith, hope, and love to one another. I believe in the best and worst parts of Dave and give him room to evolve. Dave believes in the best and worst parts of me and gives me room to evolve.

Several weeks ago, after a small squabble, I half-jokingly told Dave that I thought he knew more about my Fourness than I did. We laughed when I said it, but in many ways, this is true. Dave has had a front row seat to my life, observing more than anyone else how I live, what I live for, and why I am the way I am. Richard Rohr, in *The Enneagram: A Christian Perspective*, says that "the gift, or fruit of the spirit of a redeemed Four is balance." I can honestly say I've done a lot of work to bring my emotional life into balance (this work is lifelong), but in the course of our relationship, Dave has cultivated soil for this Four's soul to experience genuine harmony and peace. I am married to a true peacemaker.

Reflect on some of your closest friendships or relationships. Which numbers do you typically feel the safest
with? What qualities do these individuals possess that
give you room to be your full self?

THINGS MADE CLEAR

I WOKE UP TO FIND THE MOUNTAINS near my home bathed in flames. The air was polluted with smoke, ash, and toxins that made it difficult to breathe. Our sun had become an eerie orange color, a constant reminder that something was wrong. The clear blue skies that normally greeted us had been replaced with a thick, unyielding fog of hazy smoke.

Like many Fours, I struggle with anxiety. Although I feel deeply connected to suffering, when faced with overwhelming circumstances, I tend to compartmentalize, romanticize, and individualize. I can wield my privilege to stay insular and inward, closing my eyes to the pain of those who are marginalized, othered, and oppressed. I am complicit in fanning the flames of dissidence, causing further harm and chaos to our world.

Climate change is directly connected to the racism, capitalism, patriarchy, and colonization that harm the most vulnerable people across our globe. Although indigenous communities teach us that sharing natural resources is necessary for all inhabitants of this planet to flourish, we continue to hoard at the expense of marginalized people and communities both internationally and locally. The countries most impacted by systematic oppression are those now being hit hardest by climate change.

We must return to our biblical ancestors' call to lovingly steward creation with God. As "gardeners," we can no longer "dim" our eyes. As children of God, we must work toward making our beloved earth whole, just, and *clear* . . . in the light of Jesus' glory and grace.

I am fighting against my inclination, as a Four, for prolonged melancholy that perpetuates complicity. I can move from anxiety to action, shifting away from self-absorption toward collaboration within a community of individuals who are resolved to take care of our earth. I do not need to be stuck in my feelings or paralyzed by the magnitude of systemic shifts necessary for change. Like my young niece who dreams of planting beautiful gardens one day, I can embody hope and commit to change, no matter how small.

I do not need to run so far ahead into the future that I give up altogether.

Reflect on some ways you can care for God's creation on a daily basis.

What is one way you can move from self-absorption to action?

NO ENTRY, ONE WAY

THERE IS A RETREAT CENTER I often go to for soul care. As I approach, I pass a sign on the road that says, "No entry, one way." I have come to see this sign as a metaphor for my life in ministry, motherhood, and leadership. If I can feel the undercurrent of control, comparison, insecurity, and distraction welling up within me, it's time for me to explore the "no entry, one way" path again. I cannot continue on the road because I've become a hazard to others and to myself.

As a Four, social media is an easy pacifier to numb my desire for connection. Without regular breaks from it, I feed my addictive patterns of experiencing intimacy and belonging in counterfeit ways, and I begin to genuinely believe my phone is central to my life (i.e., "needing" my phone every waking moment) instead of my phone being merely a helpful accessory. When I find myself reaching for my phone more than I'm reaching for God, it is a problem of my soul.

Some of us are afraid of the stillness and silence, uncertain of who or what we are without the barrier of noise we've curated for ourselves. For others of us, silence has been a place of oppression—we've been silenced or have perpetuated injustice with our silence.

For me, "No entry, one way" means to hear God's invitation: "Be still, and know that I am God" (Psalm 46:10). "Be still" means to create space and margin in my soul by minimizing the noise and distraction that come with social media.

Instead of being run over by our hurried, frenetic schedules, we reclaim our rest as good, holy, and necessary. We reclaim our rest by opening our souls to God's presence regularly and intentionally. We allow God to tend to our wounds, our weariness, our exhaustion, to speak truth into our circumstances. In rest, we reorient ourselves as people of justice, mercy, and hope. In accepting God's invitation for rest, we embrace the opportunity to become whole.

Take some time to intentionally unplug from your technology this week. Create space for God to tend to your body, mind, heart, and soul.

SEEKING BEAUTY

OVER THE COURSE OF MY LIFE, I have noticed a pattern—I seek out beauty or art to work through unresolvable emotions or to express my own inadmissible pain. One of my earliest memories of seeking beauty in unexpected places was during my elementary years. I must have been seven or so and my family had a sweetgum tree in our backyard. I lovingly called it my "star tree" because of the star-shaped leaves bursting from its branches.

During a particularly difficult season for my family, my parents were often at odds with each other—consumed with the stress of financial strain and my father's struggle with alcoholism. I would go outside to our backyard and allow the sun's shining presence to comfort me. I would sit beside my star tree (which I believed was the only one that existed on the planet!), close my eyes, and allow the chitter-chatter of the leaves to whisper to me. I'd lie down and look up to see the vast greenery swaying with the wind. I would imagine the looming branches and starry shadows protecting and shielding me. Over time I'd become one with the tree, dancing with its leaves and swirling around in its starry force field. When I'd go back into my house, I was transformed by this encounter with beauty.

Seeking and finding beauty has been a sort of escape portal—I can imagine and discover life anew in any circumstance. It's as though a survival technique has become a superpower. Listening to a beautiful song, lighting a candle and creating a calming atmosphere, going on a long nature walk, or simply watching a friend meticulously prepare a good meal has brought healing and relief to the many dimensions of emotional intensity I have felt as a Four. Beauty has been a shield, an outlet, a comfort.

Over time, I've come to see that my ability to seek and find beauty is not a form of escapism—it is actually one of the main ways God speaks and tends to my soul. It is a direct connection to my Fourness. I grew up drawing lines between what was considered traditionally "sacred" and "secular," but I am more and more convinced that God *calls out* to me through beauty and art. Indeed, the moments with beauty that healed, nurtured, and held me all these years were, in actuality, the outstretched arms of God.

What roles do beauty, art, and creative expression play in your life?

If you are a Four, how have beauty and art been a resting or healing space for your soul?

WATER FOR MY SOUL

A COMMON SENTIMENT shared among my friends who are Fours is our yearning to be known in the no-holds-barred way we know and care for the people around us. We tend to pour out so much emotionally that we fall into self-indulgent behaviors that end up being more harmful than helpful. When I recently found myself in a self-indulgent rut, my mom took me aside and told me I needed to go to the Korean bathhouse. She said she would watch my kids, pressed the admittance ticket into my hand, and said in Korean, "Take care of yourself and go."

I never thought I would find an intersection between the bathhouse and my understanding of soul care. But as I peeled back the layers of culture, I discovered that for my mom's generation and those preceding, the bathhouse had been one of the few spaces of exhale and rest available to Korean women in an oppressive patriarchal culture devastated by years of war and colonization. The bathhouse was a place where generations of women could find rest for their weary bodies.

Communal bathing in Korea originated in the scarcity of resources in a land ravaged by centuries-long wars. Out of necessity, Koreans discovered sustainable methods of efficient and meticulous cleaning for the young and the old—women, men, and children. Today's bathhouse encompasses a gender-separated experience of communal cleansing and detoxification that involves soaking and preparing oneself in very hot water to release toxins and *ddeh-mi-ruh*, scrubbing off the dead skin cells to thoroughly cleanse the body.

As an empath, and as someone who thrives on deep connection and meaning, I was longing to be with other *halmuhnis*, *unnies*, *ddals*, and *ahjummas*—grandmothers, sisters, daughters, women—who, like me, were coming to the bathhouse for refuge, for cleansing, and for rest from their struggles. This communal, embodied, and intergenerational experience was a balm to my deep sense of isolation.

I have found it critical to distinguish my self-indulgent behaviors (selfish care) from restorative practices (soul care). For Fours, selfish care can look like self-care on the outside but is in reality an exercise of entitlement that ultimately harms the people around us. Soul care, on the other hand, brings holistic, restorative care to our entire being that overflows into being a healing presence to others.

Take time to write out some individual and communal practices that bring you restoration. What is one way you can intentionally care for your soul this week?

HANSOOM AND GENERATIONAL GRIEF

FOURS ARE IN TOUCH WITH their own suffering and therefore are unafraid to hold space for the lament, despair, and loss that others experience.

Recently, my great-aunt told me a story about the Korean War. She is a petite woman, the younger sister of my mother's mother. She is now in her eighties, frail, with her life story woven into the lines of her face. She had never once mentioned the war to me. It was an unspoken rule in our family that we did not talk about the past—the war that devastated and ripped our family apart; death shadowing them as they traveled; the attempts to escape danger; the piercing hunger, suffering, and trauma they will never forget.

My great-aunt was only a young girl when the North was invaded by communists. One day thunderous explosions shook her village. She remembers how frightened she was, how she began to hear loud popping sounds and screams of horror. Her family grabbed what they could and ran. Those who tried to flee could be killed, kidnapped, or tortured, but to stay, they knew, was also a death sentence. They boarded a boat in the middle of the night and traveled illegally to the South, tying rolled towels around the mouths of the children to silence them.

They made it safely to the South, but their long journey was just starting as they walked on foot from town to town seeking safe shelter. During one treacherously long day of travel, my great-grandmother, who was carrying her daughter's baby, lost sight of her family and disappeared. After months of searching, my family finally tracked down the village where my great-grandmother had eventually settled. When they arrived, the villagers told them the baby had died of starvation. My great-grandmother blamed herself for the death of her grandchild and the loss of her family and died of heartache.

My family's story is not unique—hundreds of thousands of Koreans shared these experiences during the Korean War. Many died from starvation and heartbreak. Many families were ripped apart by the thirty-eighth parallel and indiscriminate demarcation, never to see each other again. Babies were separated from mothers, wives from husbands, sisters from brothers, aunts from uncles—so much devastation, so much anguish.

My great-aunt holds her hands tightly as she tells me this story, the loss of her own mother and her sister. She presses her lips together and the lines on her forehead become deeper still. She breathes deeply to compose herself. Breathe in, breathe out. Every breath matters.

I believe that when my great-aunt shared this story, she finally exhaled with memories of the living dead. In Korean, we call this collective breath *hansoom*. *Hansoom* is a heavy, groaning sigh of generational grief. It implies that our grief is not individual but collective, and we exhale, groaning together, with all creation.

Fours are tethered to the interconnectedness of this collective grief. When we get in touch with our very breath, we realize that our own suffering bears witness to a communal breath of empathy. *Hansoom* is expressed alongside those in our world who are holding in cries of frustration, despair, and grief, our common humanity shared as we exhale.

> Find a quiet space and be still. Place your feet flat on the ground, close your eyes, and deeply inhale, filling your lungs with air, then release your breath, pushing the air out of your body. Breathe in the peace and restoration of God. Become mindful of the deepest parts of yourself. Reach back into your family story and history and remember the Spirit of God interceding on your behalf (Romans 8:26). Exhale the generational pain and suffering that lives in you, passing through you, the blood and tears of your ancestors. Your individual breath is a communal inhale, exhale, as God sees you, releases you, lifts you up and out of your worldly suffering. Breathe in, breathe out.

YOU ARE BELOVED

WHO AM I? AND AM I LOVED? are questions that resurface over the course of our lives. For Fours, these core questions might be reframed, Am I special? and Do I belong? We wonder if we are enough or if we need to be more or less than we actually are.

In Luke 3, John baptizes Jesus in the Jordan River. As Jesus is praying, the heavens open up and the Holy Spirit descends on him in the form of a dove. A voice from heaven speaks over Jesus, saying, "You are my Son, whom I love; with you I am well pleased" (Luke 3:22).

Henri Nouwen in his book *Life of the Beloved* says God sings this same declaration of love and belonging over each one of us: "You are my beloved child! I'm so pleased with you!" Throughout our lives, voices of criticism and rejection will challenge this Voice, shouting out that we are only what we have, what we do, or what others say about us. Competing cultural messages will consistently and persistently call out there is only room for a few to be chosen or loved. However, there is no scarcity in God's economy. Our truest and most unshakeable identity is the beloved of God.

Over the years I've been working to hear the clear, abundant, singing voice of God over me—that, indeed, I am the beloved child of God. In order to fully thrive and live a whole life, I am actively uprooting internalized narratives of shame, oppression, comparison, and rejection while fighting against outer narratives of dehumanization, distortion, diminishment, and erasure.

If you are struggling to answer the questions Who am I? and Am I loved? and wondering if as a Four, you are special enough or worthy of belonging, may you hear God's singing voice over you today and every day: "You are my beloved child, and I am so pleased with you!"

Let yourself rest for a few minutes with no agenda. Listen for the silence and stillness that is present between your thoughts. In this attentive place, you'll begin to notice your false and true self, as well as God's loving presence with you.

Take some time to notice any false tendencies that arise—any disguise, mask, narrative, or identity you've been functioning in other than your true identity as an unconditionally beloved child of God. Take a few minutes to write out your thoughts and reflections.

Take some time to notice how God is loving you right now based on your simply being in God's presence. In this place of being held in Divine embrace, let the tears fall if they come. Slowly breathe in and out a few times. Exhale your exhaustion, confusion, grief, and fear. Inhale God's tender love, grace, and peace. You are the beloved of God, and nothing can take this identity away from you.

How might God be inviting you to life and hope today? Write down your reflections and allow God to tend to your soul.

ACKNOWLEDGMENTS

I WANT TO THANK THE PEOPLE who brought this book to life. Thank you to my sister, Susan, for living these stories with me, for your belief in my words, and your invaluable edits throughout the entirety of the project. Although I still think of you as the "real writer" in our family, I know your love for the written word shaped and nurtured my own. Thank you for everything, Unnie. I love you.

Thank you to my mother, Yi Myung Eun, and my father, Yi Chong Gil, for modeling a life of sacrifice, joy, and perseverance. Your unconditional love, faithful devotion to God, and embodied resilience shaped the words on these pages. 엄마 and 아빠, I honor you. 사랑해요.

Thank you to my loving husband and partner, Dave, for your faith, encouragement, and belief in me—for taking on additional work and sacrificing so I could write without distraction. I love you; thank you for caring so well for my heart.

My incredible children, Sammy and Ellie—you are Umma's soul and inspiration. Thank you for understanding whenever Umma had to take time away to write. Your laughter, joy, assurance, and pride in this book and in me carried me to the last pages.

Thank you to my family: my brother-in-law, Albert, my beloved in-laws, 어머님, 아버님, John, Chrissy, James, Bona, and specifically Daniel for your help with Sammy and Ellie so

I could spend time writing. My beautiful nieces, Alison and Amanda—you are the next generation of Asian American female leaders, and you are going to change the world.

I want to express my deepest gratitude to my gifted editor, Cindy Bunch, who believed in my voice and writing when we met eight years ago. Thank you for taking a chance on a new author and encouraging me in the fullness of my Fourness. Thank you for amplifying the voices of women of color—this book would not have been possible without you.

Thank you to Suzanne Stabile for your honest feedback and enthusiastic guidance, and for sharing your Enneagram wisdom so generously and graciously with me.

They say a book is written in community, and this has been true for me. To my dear friends and family: I don't have the words to fully convey my gratitude for you, my community, who held me up, encouraged, championed, and loved me through the process. Thank you for believing in me, seeing me, praying for me. Thank you for showing up for my family so faithfully. I thank God for each of you.

Last, my fellow Asian American sisters and women of color: for those of us who have yet to be represented in mainstream Enneagram literature, my hope is that the stories and perspectives shared here bring some semblance of healing, pride, solidarity, and freedom in your unique journey as image bearers of God. You are beloved, valued, glorious, and powerful. Thank you for existing.

ENNEAGRAM
DAILY REFLECTIONS

SUZANNE STABILE,
SERIES EDITOR